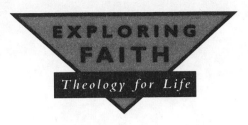

SERIES EDITORS: Leslie J Francis and Jeff Astley

USING THE BIBLE
Studying the Text

Robert Evans

DARTON · LONGMAN + TODD

First published in 1999 by
Darton, Longman and Todd Ltd
1 Spencer Court
140-142 Wandsworth High Street
London SW18 4JJ

ISBN 0-232-52344-4

A catalogue record for this book is available from the British Library.

Designed by Sandie Boccacci
Phototypeset in Minion by Intype London Ltd
Printed and bound in Great Britain by
Page Bros, Norwich, Norfolk

CONTENTS

ACKNOWLEDGEMENTS

My grateful thanks to colleagues, Ruth Ackroyd, Jean Armstrong, Eric Christianson, Andrew Dawson and Diane Hughes for help with the content or style of various of the chapters.

Quotations from the Bible are from the *New Revised Standard Version* unless otherwise indicated.

PREFACE

At the beginning of the third millennium a new mood is sweeping through the Christian churches. This mood is reflected in a more radical commitment to discipleship among a laity who wish to be theologically informed and fully equipped for Christian ministry in the secular world.

Exploring Faith: theology for life is designed for people who want to take Christian theology seriously. Taken seriously, Christian theology engages the mind, involves the heart, and seeks active expression in the way we live. Those who explore their faith in this way are beginning to shape a theology for life.

Exploring Faith: theology for life is rooted in the individual experience of the world and in the ways through which God is made known in the world. Such experience is related to and interpreted in the light of the Christian tradition. Each volume in the series takes a key aspect of theology, and explores this aspect in dialogue with the readers' own experience. Each volume is written by a scholar who has clear authority in the area of theology discussed and who takes seriously the ways in which busy adults learn.

The volumes are suitable for all those who wish to learn more about the Christian faith and ministry, including those who have already taken Christian basic courses (such as *Alpha* and *Emmaus*) and have been inspired to undertake further study, those preparing to take theology as an undergraduate course, and those already engaged on degree programmes. The volumes have been developed for individuals to work on alone or for groups to study together.

Already groups of Christians are using the *Exploring Faith: theology for life* series throughout the United Kingdom, linked by an exciting initiative pioneered jointly by the Anglican dioceses, the Board of Education of the Church and World Division and the Ministry Division of the Archbishops' Council of the Church of England, the National

Society and the Church Colleges. Used in this way each volume can earn credits towards one of the Church Colleges' Certificates and provide access to degree level study. Further information about the Church Colleges' Certificate Programme is provided on page 134.

The Church Colleges' Certificate Programme integrates well with the lifelong learning agenda which now plays such a crucial role in educational priorities. Learning Christians can find their way into degree-bearing programmes through this series *Exploring Faith: theology for life* linked with the Church Colleges Certificates.

In preparing a series of this kind, much work is done behind the scenes. Financial and staff support have been generously given by the Ministry Division. Thanks are due to Marilyn Parry for the vision of bringing together the Aston materials and the Anglican Church Colleges of Higher Education. Thanks also should go to the Aston staff and the original authors for being willing to make the materials available for reworking. We are also grateful for financial support from the following Church Colleges: Chester College; Christ Church University College, Canterbury; The College of St Mark and St John, Plymouth; St Martin's College, Lancaster; Trinity College Carmarthen; and Whitelands College (Roehampton Institute). Without the industry, patience, perception, commitment and skill of Ruth Ackroyd this series would have remained but a dream.

The series editors wish to express their personal thanks to colleagues who have helped them shape the series identity, especially Diane Drayson, Ros Fane, Evelyn Jackson, Anne Rees and Morag Reeve, and to the individual authors who have produced high-quality text on schedule and so generously accepted firm editorial direction. The editorial work has been supported by the North of England Institute for Christian Education and the Centre for Theology and Education at Trinity College Carmarthen.

Leslie J Francis
Jeff Astley

INTRODUCTION

A key premise for this book is that for Christians to read the Bible in such a way, or in such ways, as to be able to use it faithfully, they need to be open to a number of matters, such as the nature of the texts, the nature of the language used and the different approaches employed within our own tradition and outside it.

A book of this size can only begin to outline and illustrate some of these matters, but it attempts to do just that – outline and illustrate – and it uses familiar texts to give readers the opportunity to develop insights into their own reading and use of the texts and also into how and why other readers might read and use them differently. The plurality of possible readings, and of different interpretations used in different locations of Christian tradition, is offered as a positive insight for Christian use of scripture.

After opening up questions of how the Bible is used (chapter 1), there is a survey of key issues of text and translation, and of the history of interpretation of the Bible (chapter 2). There is a chapter on key concepts and methods in reading the Old Testament and the New Testament. The nature of religious language is explored in chapter 5, and then two chapters which investigate, with examples, some of the key methods of interpretation: historical approaches and literary approaches. Two chapters then discuss the relationship of interpreting biblical text with religious belief and with other ideologies. The last chapter draws together some of the approaches discussed in a worked example of interpretation, focusing on a passage in the Gospel of Mark.

The book is not a survey of the contents of the Bible, though it should help the reader to survey those contents. It is not a survey of approaches to biblical interpretation, though it opens a range of these to brief investigation and prepares the reader for further investigation and application of these. It is an introduction to using the Bible with the tools of an educated reader and with the faith of a Christian. The text includes reflective and other exercises as illustrations and worked examples of the matters under investigation.

1. OPENING UP THE BIBLE

Introduction

This chapter introduces some of the concerns that will be explored more fully in individual subsequent chapters. It opens up questions preliminary to 'How do we study the text and use the Bible?', namely, 'What is the Bible?' and 'Use of the Bible'. The authority of the Bible for Christians is recognised as a key issue both preceding and following on from other questions. A brief evaluation of some modern translations of the Bible is offered as a guide to the key resource in the studies to be made.

Reflecting on experience
Consider your experience of books and reading.

What role(s) do books and reading play in your life? For example, do you use books for information, guidance, recreation, study, escapism, personal growth?

Does your use of the Bible resemble these other experiences? If your experience of the Bible is different, what makes it different? For example, is it the context (use in church or in Bible study group), or your beliefs about it, or the nature of the texts themselves?

What is the Bible?

The 'Bible' as a name comes from the Greek *biblia* which means books. The plural term reminds us that the Bible is a collection of separately written texts, brought together over a period of time and later recognised as a closed collection, a 'canon', shared by members of a religious tradition.

The Old Testament books were almost all written originally in Hebrew and written down through about a 1,000-year period from c. 1000 to c. 160 BCE, but some of the stories in them may have been composed from 2000 BCE. The books may be differently grouped as a 'canon' in different traditions, and given different titles. Chapter 3 explores these matters further.

The Apocrypha or Deutero-canonical books are Jewish books too but ones which are not in the 'canon' of the Tanakh (Jewish Bible), and not in the Old Testament canon of all Christian churches. They were included (in Greek) in the Christian canon of the Old Testament in the fourth century CE because Christians used them as part of the scriptures they drew on. The Protestant church usually put them in the Apocrypha, separate from the Old Testament; the Catholic church includes them in the body of the Old Testament. Again, the books may be differently named and ordered in each tradition. This book will not make much reference to these texts.

Though the New Testament texts are not part of the Jewish Bible they were of course written mostly by Jews. They were written in Greek over a short period of time: from late 40s CE to perhaps 120s CE. The letters of Paul are the first recorded Christian writings; the Gospels, in the form we have them, may date from the late 60s CE (Mark) to the end of the first century (John). Chapter 4 explores these matters further.

The choice of texts for the canon of Christian scripture is considered briefly in chapter 2.

Very few of the biblical books state who their author is. Many traditions about authorship are legendary or suppositional, and were attached to the texts at a late stage in their transmission. For example, the ascription of the Pentateuch (Genesis to Deuteronomy) to Moses is not in the text; nor are the names of the Gospel writers.

Use of the Bible

The Bible is not used in the same way by all its readers, or on all occasions. When it is read out in small sections, perhaps regulated by a 'lectionary' of readings prepared for a particular denomination of churches, there is often an attempt to trace a theme in the Bible, and to match an Old Testament passage, a New Testament letter and a Gospel reading. Something in these texts is then often 'expounded' in a sermon and reflected on in order to guide and encourage a congregation in a particular belief and way of life. In private use, a similar devotional end is often sought but perhaps more often with a daily or weekly passage from one book read sequentially. The church also asks its scholars to study the texts academically in order to confirm or challenge matters of belief and behaviour. It is used as a source for ethical reflection, church policy and for spiritual growth.

How far the Bible is properly seen as an 'instruction manual' for life is debated in different churches. That it is 'edifying' is not (in these communities at least) disputed, but how far it is essentially a book of rules where the sayings and stories can be immediately understood and directly applied to one's own life is a question to which there is a whole spectrum of different answers. An approach where any verse can be taken at random, joined to any other statement in any other book of the Bible and then followed to the letter is obviously open to results not in the spirit of either of the verses found. If your finger lands first on 2 Chronicles 33:2, 'He did what was evil in the sight of the Lord ...', and then on Luke 10:37, 'Go and do likewise', you might find yourself engaged in a lifestyle not usually thought of as reflecting biblical teaching!

If such an approach is taken, some other authority than the Bible is appealed to, such as the guidance of God's Spirit, for the verses that you find. We can make a distinction between 'what the Bible itself teaches' and 'what the Spirit of God reveals to me about the meaning'. The latter is not open to being demonstrated or falsified: it is a matter of personal belief, which can be asserted but not debated. The former can be discussed, and the grounds for supporting or challenging an interpretation can be put forward based on the manuscripts, the meaning of the Hebrew and Greek, the context of the author and the first readers, the type of literature it is, and so on.

The role of belief and of the Spirit of God is by no means diminished by this 'critical' approach. Revelation of God may take place through reading scripture but the Bible, to state the obvious, is not God. Reading its words is not an infallible transference of the knowledge of God to the human mind. If its words reveal God, then God is at work to provide that revelation. Some Christians believe that *the way* God is at work to provide that revelation involves principles such as 'infallibility' or 'inerrancy' as characteristics of the Bible itself. Other Christians hold that the Bible is no less *about* God's self-revelation, though it is made up of texts written by fallible humans struggling with their understanding of God and the human condition. For them, this is the way, or a way, that the Spirit of God works.

We should note here that there are many who read the Bible who do not see it as inspired, revelatory, holy text. It is possible to read these books as pieces of ancient literature, whose meaning is accessible to the usual tools of a reader. Christians share the tools, though they may believe there is meaning in or through the text beyond what is discoverable by literary or historical analysis.

We should note too that two Christian believers can reach different conclusions about the same text: 'You shall not murder' (Exodus 20:13) leads some Christians to believe that war and capital punishment are not available as strategies of control for Christians; others, not less Christian in their faith, believe that one or both of these are justified and moral acts. What the succeeding chapters attempt to do is to demonstrate that some of the decisions about what such a text 'means' involve skills and understanding which can be developed and discussed, not merely asserted.

EXERCISE

John Robinson (1977) described four attitudes to questioning the literal and historical truth of some of the texts of the Bible:
• the cynicism of the foolish;
• the fundamentalism of the fearful;
• the scepticism of the wise;
• the conservatism of the committed.

Our phrases often reveal our own bias. Which of the positions do you think Robinson thought preferable?

How far does one or a combination of them represent your own position?

The approach in this book

This book considers the issues of studying the biblical texts and applying them primarily from the standpoint of Christians. It is a standpoint shared by this author. It is also acknowledged that this is not a single standpoint without variation of context, perspective, belief and practice. It is further acknowledged that the texts are read outside of the Christian communities of faith, and particularly that the majority of the texts are shared by people of the Jewish faith. These standpoints are secondary for the purposes of this particular book, though insights from other communities will feed our investigation. (Some of these perspectives are discussed in chapters 3 and 8.)

The nature of the texts as authoritative and normative for Christians is not directly pursued outside of sections of this introductory chapter. It is a huge question and demands another book. Chapter 8, however, is concerned with questions of the place of faith in biblical interpretation. The issues raised by this book already threaten to burst its seams: the aim is to open topics, introduce skills, develop areas of understanding in such a way as to enable and encourage further study and enquiry when you have closed this particular book.

The chapter headings indicate the structure of the investigation. Chapter 2 gathers together some of the matters that affect the text and our reading of it before we get to it: the manuscripts, the translations, the history of Christian interpretation. Chapters 3 and 4 consider (with a brevity hardly appropriate to the weight of the material) the contents and themes of the two Testaments. Chapter 5 opens the questions preliminary to most skills of interpretation, the way words are used metaphorically in religious language. Chapters 6 and 7 illustrate two basic approaches to studying biblical texts: historical criticism and literary analysis. These are not by any means irreconcilable; most readers use a mixture of both. Chapters 8 and 9 focus more on the perspective of the reader as this affects the interpretation made: questions of faith, sex and politics are seen to have an impact on our reading. The final chapter is an attempt to consolidate some of the material and methods that you will have worked through. The balance of examples throughout probably favours the New Testament, and in particular the Gospels.

The variety of skills introduced and the range of perspectives considered is significant to the overall approach taken to studying and using these texts. They reflect the understanding that it is rarely if ever possible to say, 'This and this alone is the single, complete and wholly satisfactory meaning of this particular text.' This principle also governs the questions addressed to you, the reader: they are largely 'open' questions to which a range of responses is possible, rather than 'closed' questions where you are asked to seek a single, correct answer. If the question is primarily about content rather than opinion, or if there is a response that I would particularly like you to consider, there will sometimes be notes following the questions. Doubtless, in spite of this declared intention to open rather than closed questions of interpretation, you will detect my own views and conclusions in various matters. The intention is that nonetheless you will be able to reach your own conclusions using the skills and resources that are described. The range of further reading suggested at the close of each chapter is often an opportunity to seek the different views of other authors.

EXERCISE

Do you agree that it is rarely if ever possible to say, 'This and this alone is the single, complete and wholly satisfactory meaning of this particular text'? Is it nevertheless sometimes possible to say, 'There may be more than one *right* answer but that interpretation is definitely *wrong*'? What factors have to be considered in recognising an interpretation as valid or invalid? If you need a particular text on which to focus your response, you might consider the one used above: 'You shall not murder' (Exodus 20:13).

Some English versions of the Bible

Does it matter which translation of the Bible we use? It can make a difference to what we understand, but it also depends on what use we want to make of it.

If it is not a recent translation, it cannot have used the best available manuscript evidence. For this reason, the *King James* or *Authorised Version* (seventeenth century) has had to make textual and translation decisions that modern scholarship would question. It is often stylistically very beautiful, though the original writers of Hebrew, Aramaic and Greek were not always writing beautifully or in a literary way themselves. The translation is sometimes very close indeed to the original word order, which perhaps makes a useful 'crib' for the Greek or Hebrew text but does not always make it easy to understand in English.

The *Revised Standard Version*, published in 1952, is in a line of revisions of the tradition of the *King James* translation but using better texts, new scholarship and updated English. There are versions of the text published as the *Common Bible* and authorised for use by all the main denominations, which indicates that it is not constrained by the interpretation of just one doctrinal tradition. The *New Revised Standard*

Version (1989) is an update, both stylistically and using the latest scholarship, of the *Revised Standard Version*. It is in the tradition of (where possible) phrase-for-phrase, word-for-word translations, which makes it useful for some types of textual study. There is also a concern to preserve a measure of continuity with the traditions of English Bible translation, and the *New Revised Standard Version* keeps some time-honoured phrases (like 'hallowed' in the Lord's Prayer) even if these are not used in contemporary English outside of Christian liturgy. Part of the updating includes using gender-inclusive language about people.

While some translations have chosen as far as possible a word-for-word method, others have not. *The New English Bible* led the way in the latter method in 1961 (New Testament) and 1970 (Old Testament) and was a completely new translation in 'a contemporary idiom' rather than a reproduction of 'biblical' English. It was quite bold in places in interpreting meaning-for-meaning rather than word-for-word, which makes it refreshing but not, for some types of textual study, completely reliable. What was 'contemporary idiom' in 1960 and 1971, of course, does not always sound contemporary today. *The Revised English Bible* (1989) builds on the innovative work of *The New English Bible*, but in fact is more conservative than the earlier translation. This was partly to make it easier to read aloud in worship than *The New English Bible* proved to be, and also to gain acceptance from many of the main denominations, which it achieves. Gender-inclusive language has been preferred but not if it was judged to compromise 'scholarly integrity or English style'.

The *Good News Bible/Today's English Version* (1976) also did not attempt to reproduce sentence structure, word order or stylistic devices of the original languages: the principle is one of 'dynamic equivalence', and a deliberately limited vocabulary to be as clear and simple as possible. As we will see in chapter 5, sometimes one can argue for privileging sense over precise word-equivalence. For example, the *Good News Bible* translates Paul's metaphor of 'justification' as 'being put right with God', which loses the metaphor (which refers to a judgement made in a court of law) but makes good sense and good theology. The latest version uses gender-inclusive language about people.

There are also other principles at work in governing translation method. The *New International Version* (1973) and *The New Jerusalem Bible* (1966) each has a commitment to a Christian tradition: a conservative evangelical one for the *New International Version* and the Catholic church for the *New Jerusalem Bible*. This means that the translators were committed to an understanding of the doctrine which they believe the Bible teaches, and sought to elucidate that in their translation of it. To some extent this is surely true of every translation (everyone's faith and politics and experience informs their interpretation) but it is also possible to translate in a way which does not close off alternative meanings. Christians within a particular tradition may prefer the translation which helps them stay tuned to that tradition, but it is often interesting and enlightening to compare one version with another to see if different insights are available. (More of this is in chapter 8.)

All modern translations in most editions give some indication of their method and their tradition, usually in a preface. It is then up to the reader to make use of it in reading, devotion, study or action. Most versions are available in editions that give some indication, usually in footnotes, of some of the translation decisions made or the manuscript variants that gave them pause.

EXERCISE

📖 **Read the preface** of a modern edition of the Bible.

What statements does it make about the method and nature of this translation? For what communities and purposes is the edition produced?

Further reading

Brown, R E, Fitzmyer, J A and Murphy, R E (eds) (1990), *New Jerome Biblical Commentary*, London, Chapman. See articles such as 'Inspiration' by R Collins.

Guthrie, D and Motyer, J A (eds) (1970), *New Bible Commentary*, Leicester, IVP. See articles such as 'The authority of scripture', by G W Bromiley.

Metzger, B and Coogan, M D (eds) (1994), *Oxford Companion to the Bible*, Oxford, Oxford University Press. See articles such as 'Inspiration and Inerrancy' by W H Barnes and 'Authority of the Bible' by R Hammer.

Richardson, A and Bowden, J (eds) (1983), *New Dictionary of Christian Theology*, London, SCM. See articles such as 'Biblical criticism' by J Bowden, and 'Authority' by R C P Hanson.

2. OLD BOOKS, NEW READERS

Introduction

This chapter looks at some of the issues for a modern reader of the Bible when faced with this collection of very old writings, which have a 2,000-year history of Christian interpretation. It considers our reliance on different manuscripts, and on some of the editing processes which underlie our versions. It then looks at some of the different approaches to understanding them in the Christian church, many of which still influence the use of the Bible today.

Reflecting on experience

Have you read any other texts which are old (for example, classical literature, Shakespeare, nineteenth-century novels) or any other texts which have been translated from a different language? What makes you aware as a reader that a story was written in an older period of history? What, if anything, makes you aware that it was not first written in the language you are reading it in?

When you read a (familiar) text from the Bible, how far do you find your interpretation influenced by sermons, or lessons, or commentaries that you have heard or read before? Re-read any such text (for example, **Luke 15:11–32**). Can you recall what you have been told about this passage and by whom? How far do these things influence your understanding of it now?

Before the texts were written

Luke 1:1–4 is one of several occasions where biblical authors refer to other collections of writings (1:1) and to oral accounts (1:2) that have preceded the writing down of their own text.

As in this instance the material in our biblical books sometimes contains material from an earlier period than the author's own time. On this basis, Miriam's song in Exodus 15:21 has sometimes been referred to as 'the oldest verse in the Bible'.

There have often been stages of composition, transmission and development before stories were written down. Psalm 104, a hymn of creation, is probably earlier than our text of Genesis 1, and may have influenced the later text. Stories were sometimes collected together and then edited afresh: for example, Chronicles recasts much of the material in Samuel and Kings (like the building of Solomon's Temple in 2 Chronicles 3 which is based on 1 Kings 6).

The manuscripts

What happened next? The manuscripts we now have are not the authors' originals but copies of copies of copies. There are no surviving original manuscripts of any of the books in the Bible.

Until 50 years ago, the oldest surviving manuscripts for the Old Testament dated only from the ninth century CE, from the early medieval Masoretes (schools of Jewish scholars) who had harmonised all the texts of the Hebrew scriptures to make one 'authorised' version. When they had done this, the scholars destroyed all the variant manuscripts. (How very much modern scholars wish they had not!) However, the great find of the Dead Sea Scrolls in 1948 in the caves at Qumran has given us parts of all the Old Testament books except Esther, and these manuscript versions are much older than the Masoretic text: they date from the third century BCE to the beginning of the second century CE. But they are still not authors' originals.

The earliest surviving collections of New Testament manuscripts are the great 'codices' (books) named by the places where they were held: Codex Sinaiticus, Codex Alexandrinus, Codex Vaticanus, Codex Bezae. They date from the fourth and fifth centuries CE. There are also older papyri (papyrus leaves) containing sections of individual books in different languages. The oldest may be a piece of John's Gospel, in Coptic, from the early second century. You can see some of these in museums,

e fragments of New Testament codices from the early third cen-
Chester Beatty Museum in Dublin, or the Codex Sinaiticus in
ritish Museum in London.

Users of the Bible are reliant on textual scholars to provide the most
accurate text they can from the different manuscripts. There is no single ancient Hebrew and Greek collection translated in its entirety for
our English versions: our translations draw on all the available manuscripts which differ from one another. There are many ancient manuscripts to draw from, especially for the New Testament (over 3,000) but
again no originals.

Issues of copying

All sorts of things can happen in the copying and transmission of
manuscripts. There can be misplacement of material: individual parch-
ments or papyrus leaves can be put in the wrong order in a codex or a
scroll, or with smaller sections the eye of a copier can 'slip' so that part
of a passage is copied out of order. Notes written into the margin of a
text might be taken by the next copier as intended for inclusion in the
body of the text itself.

In deciding between two variants, there are some general principles
that sometimes help, though they are far from infallible. One is a principle of preferring (as likely to be closer to the original) 'the more
difficult reading': copiers are more likely to have tried to make sense of
a text that they do not understand than to reduce a clear expression to
something incomprehensible. Another principle is that of preferring
'the shorter reading' of two variants: the initial assumption is that
copiers tend to add material more often than leave material out. An
exception to this principle is where a copier's eyes may have 'jumped' a
line or more from a phrase in one line that is similar to one in a lower
line. Every case has to be looked at separately.

The problems of all the variations do raise a big question for those
who refer to the Bible as if it were a precisely defined source of the exact
'words of God', understood through literal knowledge and accuracy,
rather than offering the reader, in its parts or as a whole, an encounter
with 'the word of God', apprehended through faith. If the precision of
the words is the important thing, we have to ask 'Which variants are the
"words of God" and which are not?' and this is surely unanswerable.

In the following examples of textual variants, the principle of 'the
shorter reading' may be an editor's or translator's choice, but the

additions are usually there in your version to read, nevertheless. See the 'footnotes' to these texts in most modern editions of the Bible. This is where a small letter or number by part of the text tells you there is a note at the bottom of the page about the text or about the translation.

☐ **Read John 8:1–11.** Your version probably brackets this off in some way. It has as much claim to be an authentic tradition about Jesus as any other episode in the Gospels, but it does not belong here in John's Gospel; most of the manuscripts do not have it. Some add it here, or after John 7:36, or right at the end of John's Gospel or after Luke 21:38. Some scholars suggest that it fits Luke's tradition better than John's. If the only way to preserve it for us to read was for copiers to include it in one of the Gospels, we might be grateful they did so and wonder how many other traditions are lost to us because they were not so selected.

☐ **Read Mark 16:1–8.** Then read any following verse or verses which your version gives you. There are four variants in the manuscript traditions of the end of Mark. Some finish at verse 8. One manuscript adds a short ending. Others add verses 9–20, though some mark the addition as doubtful. Others include both these additions. The style of the additions is different from that of the main body of the Gospel.

EXERCISE

Why do you think early copiers find ending Mark at 16:8 unacceptable? Do you think the first author 'Mark' could nevertheless have intended to finish on this note of 'unfinished business'? What material did the copiers use in making additions? (For example, compare Mark 16:12–13 with Luke 24:13ff, and Mark 16:15–16 with Matthew 28:19–20.)

Canons

'Canons' are official lists or collections of written works, recognised by particular authorities or communities. Different faith communities (Jewish and Christian, Catholic and Protestant) do not have identical canons of scripture. They do not have exactly the same books in their Bibles, do not put them in the same order, do not always call them by the same names and do not always order their chapters and verses in exactly the same way. The process was sometimes a long one: a work was composed, circulated, and perhaps revised. Some books were accepted before others so the canon grew before it was closed. In one of the Deutero-canonical books (see chapter 1) there may be a reference to some of the last books to be included in the canon (possibly Daniel and Esther) in the second century BCE: 'Judas … collected all the books that had been lost on account of the war … and they are in our possession' (2 Maccabees 2:14) (Beckwith, 1993).

For the New Testament canon, from the close of the first century to the middle of the second, there was a growing recognition of many of our texts as important for all Christian communities. By the end of the second century the broad base of the canon was fixed though uncertainty still existed on some books as to whether they should be out or in. Uncertainty over the inclusion of Hebrews, James and Jude in the canon persisted right through to the fourth century, as did views that other books not now in the canon *should* be included: Christian books like the *Didache* and the *Shepherd of Hermas*. The need for an authoritative decision about the canon was particularly felt because of claims by some religious groups (called 'gnostics') to have received special revelation: the church wanted to be able to say, 'Your revelations are not part of our teachings.' There were three key criteria for inclusion in the New Testament: books should have as primary source one of the first-generation 'apostles' (though it is by no means certain that they all do), they should conform to an understanding of Christian teaching called 'the rule of faith', and they should have the agreement of all the churches (du Toit, 1993).

Translation problems

Most readers of the Bible are also reliant on translators or teams of translators who have used the best manuscript versions they can and the most recent evidence for the meaning of obscure words. Some case studies follow. There is further investigation of the tasks of translation in chapter 5.

Even if we are reasonably sure of what the manuscript says, with no gaps or variants, we do not always know what it means. Footnotes at the bottom of the page in your Bible may tell you about some of these.

📖 **Read 1 Corinthians 7:21.** There is no problem with the manuscripts or with the Greek words but there are two words which could mean either of two quite opposite things about what Christian slaves should do. The Greek says, literally, 'If you can gain your freedom, prefer to use (it).' It could mean either, 'prefer to use *your present condition of slavery*' or 'prefer to use *that opportunity of freedom*'. The context does not entirely help: 7:24 suggests the first solution, but 7:23 suggests the second. The translators usually make a choice and put the one they are backing into the main text and give you the alternative as a footnote.

A textual problem and some solutions

Different versions of the Bible make different decisions about textual variants: about which manuscript to follow, what to do about unknown words or gaps in the manuscripts, how much to explain, add or harmonise. An example is the different attempts to deal with 1 Samuel 13:1. The translations are from Davies (1995).

The Masoretic (Hebrew) text of this verse could be translated literally as follows:

> Saul's age was one when he became king and he reigned two years over Israel.

There is nothing wrong in the syntax of the verse but it does seem as if something is missing. The information does not conform with other statements in the same book about Saul and his reign.

📖 **Compare these versions.** They are ancient or recent attempts to deal with an apparently erroneous text. Which strategy best helps you as a reader?

In the *Septuagint* (the third-century BCE Greek translation) this verse is left out of most manuscripts, though some give Saul's age as 'thirty'.

> Saul's age was thirty when he became king.

In the *King James Version*, the translation of this verse takes some of the Hebrew as it stands but takes the two years to apply to the action of the following verse. This is an ingenious solution though not probable in terms of original meaning.

Saul reigned one year; and when he had reigned two years over Israel ...

The *New Revised Standard Version* has a strategy to let the reader share part of the problem posed by the manuscripts. The notes indicated by *b* and *c* explain the gaps in the translation. (Note *b* is not entirely true, perhaps: it is the *right* number that is missing.)

> Saul was ...*b* years old when he began to reign; and he reigned for ... and two*c* years over Israel.
> *b* the number is lacking in the Hebrew text.
> *c* two is not the entire number; something has dropped out.

In the *New International Version*, the first of the translators' additions in brackets is a guess, based on the guess made in the Septuagint manuscripts; the second is a guess, pure and simple. Should translators guess? Can they avoid it? (The *New International Version* footnotes let the reader know what has been done.)

> Saul was (thirty years) old when he became king, and he reigned over Israel for (forty-)two years.

Saul's age and the length of his reign probably do not matter much in terms of our faith or our grasp of biblical history and theology but the example illustrates what translators and others who deal with manuscript variants (have to) do. There are many such issues dealt with by translators in many different ways, and some of them *do* impact on questions of theology and faith. The footnotes in a good modern translation, and the commentaries, should alert you to any contentious issues in manuscript or translation.

Readers, old and new

The Bible has never been used without being interpreted. The act of reading is an act of interpretation: a second person making sense in their time and place and circumstances of what one person has written in another time and place and circumstances. What follows is a very brief and very selective overview of the interpretation of the Bible. The intention is to highlight some of the interpretative methods that have influenced modern readers of the Bible, or have influenced the tradition in which we may stand.

Pre-twentieth century there is a long history of Jewish interpretation of the Hebrew scriptures. A process of interpretation can happen within the biblical texts themselves: the literary relationships of Chronicles to Samuel and Kings, and of Psalm 104 to Genesis 1, have been mentioned above.

The New Testament writers (almost all of whom were Jewish) offer some interpretation of the (Hebrew) scriptures. They were using these texts to help them understand the significance, particularly, of the death and resurrection of Jesus. The Gospel writers show Jesus himself as participating in the interpretation of the scriptures.

📖 **Read Mark 10:1–12.** Jesus here refers to Genesis 1:27 to qualify or counter the Pharisees' reference to Deuteronomy 24:1. Disputing one text with another like this was and still is a method in Jewish biblical interpretation.

EXERCISE

Jesus seems to argue that one text (Genesis 1:27) indicates the will of God in creation and that the other (Deuteronomy 24:1) is a concession to human weakness, and that the Genesis text carries more weight. Do you think this is a strategy that other users of the Bible, including ourselves, can use when two texts are in tension, or is this an example of Jesus' own interpretative authority?

📖 **Read Galatians 4:21–31.** Here Paul introduces a form of 'allegory', a non-literal symbolism, into the ways Christians interpret the scriptures. In an allegory, all the characters in a story are seen to represent other people or abstract concepts. (The story this allegory is based on is mainly in Genesis 16 and 21.)

EXERCISE

What, according to Paul's allegory, does each character (Sarah, Hagar, Isaac and Ishmael) represent?

A non-Christian Jew of the time might have rejected Paul's allegory and seen Sarah's son Isaac as the 'present Jerusalem'. Can you make a different allegory using this comparison from the same characters? This might suggest that the interpretation of allegories is subjective: what you interpret depends on your original point of view.

During the first two centuries, Christian interpretation of biblical texts was guided by practical concerns: the needs of missionary preaching, the instruction of new converts, the defence of Christianity directed at non-Christians, and arguments against 'heretical' teachings (Froehlich, 1993, p. 312). The methods included many of the traditions of Jewish interpretation and the sort of allegory used by Paul.

In the fourth century among the Greek 'fathers' there were two main schools of interpretation: that of Alexandria which promoted systematic allegorisation (cf. the example from Galatians above); and that of Antioch, which regarded the texts primarily as historical documents, but also looked for spiritual, non-literal meanings.

In the Western, Latin, tradition, writers like Augustine stress the priority of the spiritual goal of reading scripture without discouraging the investigation of the plain sense of its words. There has always been this tension between how literal is the meaning to be taken and the non-literal, spiritual significance that religious readers also find.

The medieval tradition developed a fourfold interpretation: literal, allegorical, tropological (moral) and anagogical (spiritual). If a Bible text uses the word 'Jerusalem', the medieval tradition of interpretation would explain this in four different ways, all of which should be investigated for the full meaning of the text. Probably the best way to understand this is to take an example (Froehlich, 1993, p. 314). Jerusalem in the fourfold medieval tradition is expressed as:

- *literally* the geographical and historical city;
- *allegorically* the church;
- *tropologically* the human soul;
- *anagogically* heaven or 'the heavenly city'.

EXERCISE
📖 **Read Psalm 121,** which is about Jerusalem.

How far can you interpret this psalm in the fourfold way as having meaning about the church, the soul and heaven, as well as the capital city of David's kingdom?

The establishment of universities in the thirteenth century encouraged the emphasis on systematic, literal analysis (of the Latin text) seeking to find support for the church's doctrinal theology. Thomas Aquinas is probably the best known of the 'scholastic' authors. A scholarly know-ledge of the biblical languages was not usual until much later, in the six-teenth century (Bentley, 1993).

In the Reformation movements (sixteenth century) theologians of all sides sought scriptural support for their views, and there was a focused tension between the authority of doctrine and the authority of scrip-ture. In Catholic tradition it was and is the task of the church to deter-mine the true sense of the scriptures. The Protestant Reformed traditions claimed the freedom to interpret the biblical texts without this doctrinal authority. In fact this freedom was soon limited in the Lutheran and Reformed churches too: their statements of teaching and belief, like the doctrinal authority of the Catholic church, guided or determined what interpretations were acceptable for those churches (Jeanrond, 1991).

In Britain in the seventeenth, eighteenth and nineteenth centuries, there was an intensity of conflicts over religious freedom and challenges to the church teaching. Philosophers such as Thomas Hobbes, John Locke and Isaac Newton were part of this debate. The new knowledge, and the view that the new principles of investigation were moves away from superstition and prejudice, has given the term 'Enlightenment' to the movement and, broadly, the period. Modern biblical criticism (crit-ical and historical study of the Bible) had its beginnings principally in Germany in the eighteenth century.

A second type of new learning in particular seemed to challenge the church's position on the accuracy of scripture. There was a surge of scientific work and publication in archaeology, geology and astronomy and notably in biology with Darwin's *Origin of Species* in 1859. This is where the perceived opposition between science and religion begins, though scientists and church people on both sides often argued, then as now, for the considered use of reason and scientific understanding within the interpretation of scripture.

There were scholars in the church who insisted that the new learning had to be considered, but they did so at peril of their jobs and some-times of their physical safety. Some clergy and academics published a collection called *Essays and Reviews* in 1860, in which Benjamin Jowett wrote: 'We are determined not to submit to this abominable system of terrorism which prevents the statement of the plainest facts, and makes true theology or theological education impossible ... The time has come when it is no longer possible to ignore the results of criticism' (Vidler, 1974).

Twentieth century

This century has seen both a reaction to the concerns of the preceding century and the outworkings of those same concerns. The overarching question has remained that of the historical nature or otherwise of biblical texts and the historical-critical methods used to investigate them, but perhaps most Christians in Britain today are comfortable with some forms of biblical criticism, as they are also with some types of scientific thinking. One of the *reactions*, however, was the development of Christian 'Fundamentalism' which was a group formed in 1918 in the USA, opposed both to critical biblical scholarship, and to scientific evolutionary theory. In the Catholic church, the Second Vatican Council (1960s) was a watershed for Catholic biblical scholarship, which now has a greater degree of academic independence from doctrinal controls than had been the case.

The nature of the historical-critical investigation of biblical texts has undergone changes and trends. Three major methods flourished, and still have users today: source criticism (from 1900s), form criticism (from 1920s) and redaction criticism (from 1950s). Read further in chapter 7. The 'new criticism' of 1940s/1950s in secular literary analysis was not immediately taken up in biblical studies, but since the 1970s all the methods used in secular literature can be found in biblical studies too.

Here is an attempt to map recent trends in biblical studies (Clines, 1993).

Pre 1970s: 'author-centred' reading. The meaning is that intended by the author. This is a historical-critical perspective. The key problem is whether we can know with much certainty what any author meant; and of course we do not often know who the authors of our biblical text were. (Some of the issues will be investigated in chapter 6.)

1970s: 'text-centred' reading. This understands meaning to be located on the page (cf. the secular new criticism of the 1940s). This leaves historical questions for antiquarians. It involves the study of themes, images, plot, character, style, metaphor, point of view, narrators, implied readers, etc. The problems here are both whether we can properly sever a text from its past, especially in a religious tradition that identifies itself by its response to key moments of history, and whether a text can be said to have a meaning without a reader to give it meaning. (Some of the issues will be investigated in chapter 7.)

1980s: 'reader-centred' reading. Here, meaning is determined by the reader's response. This acknowledges the reality of the reader's position, her/his interests, prejudices and ideas. There is an interest in the process of reading and the social community of the reader. The idea of a 'community of readers' is a useful one for users of the Bible: a community of readers shares some common ideas about what tools and methods are useful in interpreting its texts. (Some of the issues will be investigated in chapters 8 and 9.)

1990s: 'ideology-centred' reading. David Clines (writing in 1993) discovers and projects a growing concern for the 'ideology' of a text. Whose interests does a particular text reflect and serve? Do our interpretations empower some people and ignore or oppress others? (These issues also are pursued in chapter 9.)

The pre-1970s author-centred approach still has currency, even primacy, in academic biblical studies and in large sections of the church. Historical-critical interpretation continues to be seen by many as the central tradition. (Read further in chapter 6.)

Using the Bible at this end of a long tradition

The sections above on manuscripts, the variants and the different translations suggest, rightly, that there are areas of real uncertainty or *provisionality* in the task of using the Bible. The sections on the 2,000-year tradition of Christian interpretation demonstrate the *plurality* of interpretation that has taken place at every stage. There is no time in the tradition to which we can appeal and say, 'Ah, then the meaning was single, certain and undisputed. In that golden time, all readers took the spiritual meaning'; or 'Then, all readers took the literal meaning.' Rather, we inherit many of their methods and their readings. We have also discovered new ones.

📖 **Read one opinion.** Here is the conclusion of one biblical scholar and Christian minister, Marie Isaacs (1991), on the subject of interpreting the Bible in Christian preaching:

> (One of the important contributions of modern forms of criticism is) the insight that there is no one, definitive reading of a text. This does not imply that all readings are equally valid, but it does affirm

that, although there are certain constraints upon interpretation, the text is not thereby necessarily confined to one meaning. One of the more destructive effects of a dogmatic control of the Bible is that, by limiting its interpretation to one reading, it tends to make scripture less rather than more accessible to contemporary faith ... (A) multiple-reading approach has far more to offer the preacher than the dogmatic certainties of 'the definitive interpretation'.

EXERCISE
Do you agree with Marie Isaacs that scripture is more accessible to contemporary faith because we are not limited to a single 'definitive interpretation'? What do we lose and what do we gain by being open to more than one meaning in a text?

Further reading

Metzger, B and Coogan, M D (1993), *The Oxford Companion to the Bible*, Oxford, Oxford University Press. See articles such as 'Bible' by L Holmgren, 'Canon' by N Sarna and A du Toit, 'Manuscripts' by E Tov and B Metzger, 'History of interpretation' by J Barr.

Stacey, D (1979), *Groundwork of Biblical Studies*, London, Epworth.

Vidler, A (1974), *The Church in an Age of Revolution*, Harmondsworth, Penguin (chapter 11).

3. READING THE OLD TESTAMENT

Introduction

This chapter considers the nature of the Old Testament books and some of the approaches taken to interpret them. Jewish as well as Christian traditions of reading these texts are considered (see also chapter 8). The central idea of 'Israel, the people of God' will be used to focus some of our questions. The interpretation of the Old Testament *in* the New Testament will be investigated.

Reflecting on experience

Make a very brief note of characters, episodes or teachings from the Old Testament that you most easily remember. Can you say why these are the memorable ones?

Do you read every passage with the same attitude? For example, are the commands in **Exodus 20:1–17** and the ones in **Exodus 21:2–25** equally significant for you? Can you explain any difference in significance?

The Christian and Jewish Bibles

The Christian Bible, of course, is not the New Testament texts alone but the Old Testament and the New Testament. When the texts that now make up the New Testament were written, the sacred writings of the first-century Christian Jews and Christian Gentiles were the Hebrew scriptures. It is a Christian usage rather than a Jewish one that refers to the collections as 'Testaments'. This is an old word and the Hebrew and Greek words rendered as 'testament' are usually translated today as 'covenant'. Christians, then, have books of the Old Covenant and books of the New Covenant. The idea reflects the prophetic promise, for example, 'The days are surely coming, says the Lord, when I will make a new covenant with the house of Israel' (Jeremiah 31:31). The idea is taken up in Jesus' words in the earliest version of the Last Supper: 'This cup is the new covenant in my blood' (1 Corinthians 11:25).

Different readers will refer to this collection in different ways. The Old Testament is the traditional Christian name. The recognition that Christians share the collection with Jews (for whom it is not the 'old' part of something 'new') leads some people to refer to it as the First Testament, the Common Testament, the Hebrew Bible or the Jewish Bible. Jews themselves are more likely to refer to it as Tanakh. This is an acronym, a name made up of the first letters of the three sections in which, as Jewish scriptures, the different books are ordered: T for *Torah* (the Law/the Pentateuch), N for *Nebi'im* (the Prophets) and K for *Ketubim* (the Writings).

Implications of the ordering of the books

The canons are not arranged in order of the books having being *written*, though some are arranged in the order of the *events* they refer to.

A lot of the dating of events is disputed. Some key events, which have some consensus on dating, will be referred to in this chapter. The Exodus might reflect events of the end of the thirteenth century BCE; the reign of King David is dated to around 1000 BCE and the foundation of the Temple to 967 BCE; the deuteronomic reforms are dated to the seventh century BCE and the Babylonian exile from 587–539 BCE.

As for the composition of the books, there are two types of questions about dating: 'How old is the material in them?' and 'At what time did they take the form in which we have them now?' and both questions are much disputed. Ancient poems probably provide the earliest surviving literature included in various books: for example, the Song of Deborah in Judges 5 may well be contemporary with the twelfth-century events it describes, whereas the Book of Judges as a whole was very probably not composed until five centuries later. As we saw in chapter 2, many books in the Bible contain material that existed in oral or written form before being collected in our books, but all of the books in their present form probably date from after 1000 BCE. Some scholars give Daniel as the last to be written, in the 160s BCE.

The different names and the different categorising of the books in different canons is a clue that this collection of books is read and understood differently by different people. Compare the Christian ordering with the Jewish:

The Jewish Tanakh

Torah (Pentateuch)	Genesis to Deuteronomy;
Nebi'im (Prophets)	former – Joshua, Judges, Samuel, Kings; latter – Isaiah, Jeremiah, Ezekiel and the twelve minor prophets;
Ketubim (Writings)	Psalms, Proverbs, Job, Song of Songs, Ruth, Lamentations, Ecclesiastes, Esther, Daniel, Ezra, Nehemiah, Chronicles.

The Christian Old Testament

Pentateuch	Genesis to Deuteronomy;
Historical books	Joshua, Judges, Ruth, Samuel, Kings, Chronicles, Ezra, Nehemiah, Esther;
Poetic books	Job, Psalms, Proverbs, Ecclesiastes, Song of Songs and Lamentations (Lamentations is put after Jeremiah);
Prophets	Isaiah, Jeremiah, Ezekiel, Daniel and the twelve minor prophets.

The absence of a category of historical books from the Tanakh, or the inclusion of this category in the Old Testament, may indicate a difference in how these books may be viewed.

Christian tradition tends to see a structural principle of the 'salvation-history' of the Old Testament leading to a fulfilment in the work and person of Christ. The promise to Abraham, 'In you all the families of the earth shall be blessed' (Genesis 12:3) is seen as a key event, and the thread of the history runs through the kingship and 'royal house' of David, whose son built a Temple where God might 'dwell on the earth' (1 Kings 8:27), a Temple which is destroyed and then rebuilt (Ezra 3:10–13). The New Testament writers see the promise to Abraham fulfilled through Christ, so that Christians become 'the children of the promise' to Abraham (Romans 9:8); and Jesus, 'son of David' (Romans 1:3), himself replaces the 'Temple' (John 2:21). This is a very particular idea giving an order and character to books that cover many events and many ideas, and which could be seen as revealing other 'patterns' as well or instead.

In the ordering of the Tanakh, the 'historical' books are all there but divided among the sections of prophets and writings. Some of the ordering reflects a liturgical use: an annual cycle of festivals rather than a linear history leading up to the end and fulfilment of that history. The writings contain the five scrolls called 'Megilloth' read in a lectionary cycle at the Jewish feasts:

- The Song of Songs is read at Passover (as a message of God's love for Israel);
- Ruth is read at Pentecost (reflecting the harvest theme);
- Lamentations is read at the Ninth of the Month of Ab (a fast day commemorating the destruction of Jerusalem and of the Temple);
- Ecclesiastes is read at Sukkot (the Feast of Booths, commemorating the temporary dwellings of the long passage through the wilderness);
- Esther is read at Purim (commemorating the salvation of the Jews recorded in that book).

No less than Christianity, Judaism reflects a strong sense of history and salvation-history, but this arrangement of the books shows that the Tanakh is also understood to be 'about' the continuity of God's relationship with Israel, and the awareness in Judaism of needing to recall and relive parts of that history.

The books can be read in these interrelating, sequential ways (a reading sometimes called 'canonical' criticism) or they may be studied as individual books, with individual messages.

EXERCISE

📖 **Read Lamentations 1 and 5.** In the Old Testament this collection of songs comes after Jeremiah, and was traditionally associated with his prophecies of the desolation of Jerusalem at the hands of the armies of Babylon. In the Tanakh, it is part of a cycle of readings in the *Ketubim* and read at a festival (see above) lamenting the destruction of the Temple that remains destroyed today.

In one canonical ordering an historical situation is primary, and in the other a present situation. What difference might this positioning of Lamentations make to how you read and understand it?

The people of God

The Old Testament or Tanakh contains the books of a nation, and they are profoundly about that nation and its covenant relationship with God. The nation Israel is perhaps defined by *its* God ('I am the LORD your God ... you shall have no other gods before me', Exodus 20:2–3) and by the claim, enshrined in that relationship, to two things in particular. One of these is *land* ('To your offspring I will give this land', Genesis 12:7, ' ... the land of Canaan, which I am giving to the Israelites for a possession', Deuteronomy 32:49). Another is *family* ('You shall keep my covenant, you and your offspring after you throughout their generations', Genesis 17:9). These core measures of identity, with their historical and theological claims, are reflected in the concerns of the books of the nation, and of course remain crucial to much of the history and present reality of Jews throughout the world, and of the present-day inhabitants of Israel.

The scope of the Old Testament is huge: it has, for example, sexual love poetry (the Song of Songs), codes of law and holiness (Leviticus), stories of God bartering with an old man (Genesis 18), dramatic political histories (Esther), proverbial wisdom (Proverbs), sceptical wisdom in the face of an unpredictable world (Ecclesiastes) and apocalyptic visions (Daniel). A small nation can have wide-ranging views and disparate experiences, as well as definitive experiences relating to national identity.

The bringing together of these books therefore defies any single schematisation but three events are sometimes recognised as in some way definitive for the identity and self-understanding of the people Israel. Two are the great movements of the people, in the exodus from Egypt and the exile to Babylon. These are archetypally the experiences of pilgrimage and promise, exile and return, which inform many of the books. The third event that perhaps describes, or existentially defines, Israel is the story of when that name was first given to a man whose name was taken by the nation.

EXERCISE

📖 **Read Genesis 32:22–32.** As your Bible's footnotes probably tell you, Israel means 'one who strives with God' or 'God strives'; and Peniel means 'the face of God'.　　　　　　▶▶

> If a nation tells this story about its ancestor and hero, what char-
> acteristics does it seem that the nation values? What does the
> nation Israel share with the man who is here first called by this
> name?

This is one of those stories in a biblical book that is older than the book. It may have gone through many changes and retellings through genera- tions of story-tellers. In some ways it is a 'primitive' story in picturing God as a man, and a man who is apparently nearly defeated, and more- over as a being who must leave before the day breaks. In other ways it is not so much 'primitive' as 'primal' in reflecting something profoundly significant about the human condition and our spirituality. It contains experiences of faith that the reader may share with Jacob, with the ear- liest tellers of the story and with the writer(s) who included it in the Book of Genesis. This story can be seen as the story not so much, or not just, of the man Jacob, but of the nation Israel: a nation that is persis- tent, striving, blessed, preserved, crippled, triumphant, a people who 'struggle with God till the break of day'.

Some critical approaches

The trends in biblical interpretation s   l in chapter 2 are all reflected in the approaches taken to the   ament.

Historical-critical reading

Study of the Old Testament in the weste   emic and Christian tra- dition has often centred on the historic   l approach. The histor- ical sequence from Abraham through t   turn from exile and the rebuilding of the Temple is seen as the fou   tion for study of the texts. The texts have then been studied in the context of that history, often with an emphasis on source criticism and concerned with questions of the origins of a text, compilation, date and authorship. (There is more about this approach, though with a focus on the New Testament, in chapter 6.)

This remains a key approach to reading the Old Testament. The texts, as we have seen, were written over roughly a 1,000-year span and refer to the history and faith of that period and of the 1,000 years before that. In that time the culture and experiences of the people changed. An

investigation of the historical and social setting of a text may help readers grasp an interpretation of the text that otherwise would not be open
to them. Moreover the text is telling us about *two* historical periods: for
example, the Book of Judges reflects preoccupations of the writer/com-
pilers in the seventh century BCE as well as the events and sources of the
thirteenth to eleventh centuries, the time of the Judges. The historical-
critical approach investigates both.

Sociological perspectives

This approach is a more recent development but it is related to the
historical-critical approach in a concern to investigate the life of
the people *behind* the text. Questions are asked such as, 'What was the
structure of the society at different periods in Israel's history?' and
'What roles did people take in society?' For example, a study of the role
of the prophet in society, using sociological categories, might ask
whether this role led the prophet to support the *status quo* with words
of divine approval, or to critique the society and counter the will of the
king with a view of the will of God.

EXERCISE
📖 Read 2 Samuel 7:1–17 and 12:1–15.

What does the stance of the prophet Nathan seem to be with
respect to the monarchy? How far does his prophetic role support
David's kingship and how far does it challenge it? On what
grounds is any criticism made?

Literary approaches

In recent years there has been a flourishing of approaches for which the
historical origin of the events, the historical or sociological setting of
the writers, and the relation of the ideas to Christian or Jewish theology are not the object of the investigation. The interest is in the 'final
form' of the text as we have it now, rather than its sources and authorship. The wealth of types of literature in the Old Testament and the
various narrative genres of saga, myth, satire, parable, chronicle and
so on (some wide-ranging and some sharply focused, shaped and
polished) offer an exciting field of study for anyone with an appreciation of story and literature. (More of this is found in chapter 7.)

Ideological criticism

This very recent emphasis in biblical interpretation moves beyond, or behind, interpretative description of the texts to evaluation of the interpretation itself. There is a focus on the social and political interests expressed in a text and those same interests as they impact on the reader and interpreter of the text. The perspective of people, both the characters in the text and people reading the texts, who are disadvantaged by poverty and attitudes to race and gender is made central to the interpretative task. (More of this is found in chapter 9.)

The presence of themes of liberation and social justice in the Old Testament favours this approach. Such themes are found particularly in the exodus and the eighth-century prophets.

EXERCISE

📖 Read Amos 6:1–8 and 8:4–8. The prophet tells us in 1:1 that his own social condition is not high or wealthy.

What significance might be found in these passages by a community of
• poor Christians;
• wealthy Christians?

How far do you think that the church has interpreted texts like this from the perspective of the poor?

'Reading the gaps'

A recognition relating to literary and ideological criticisms is that there is a wealth of opportunity for *speculation*. There are characters in the stories whose personalities are only hinted at and whose motives are not explained; there are people who are mentioned but who do not speak and whose views we do not hear; there are events that must have taken place but which are not narrated. Every reader 'fills in' some of these details in making sense of the text. The more historical and sociohistorical study we have made, the more our speculations are likely to reflect the context of the story or of its first readers.

This approach recognises that a reader is 'constructing' the reading of the text, not merely 'discovering' it ready-made in all its details. Some of these constructions can become elaborate works of literature or art in their own right. Milton's epic poem *Paradise Lost* is, among other things, a retelling of parts of Genesis 2 and 3 that 'fills in' action, dialogue, description and explanation. An etching by Rembrandt depicts (as have many painters before and since) the man, the woman and the serpent of Genesis 3, and in doing so 'reveals' or 'adds' expression, characterisation, indications of motive and meaning. Cecil B de Mille's *The Ten Commandments*, or Dreamworks' animated film *The Prince of Egypt*, retell the biblical narratives with background incidents, details and dialogue that may be interpreting the biblical text and may be replacing it with a different 'text' which has a different meaning.

Both Old Testament and New Testament have been rich sources for artists and writers to 'read the gaps'. There has been a flourishing of 'cultural studies' examining how these works are both informed by and influence interpretation of the Bible. An ideological approach can make an evaluation of these acts of interpretation.

EXERCISE

Choose an example from art, sculpture, cinema or literature which is an interpretation of a biblical text, for example, a reproduction of a painting of a biblical incident.

Compare it with a reading of the biblical text. What 'gaps' have been filled? Does the characterisation of any of the figures indicate creative speculation based on the text but not explicit in the text? Does it seem to tell the same story or is there a fundamental change?

Critical approaches among Jews and Christians

Modern biblical scholarship is neither Jewish nor Christian but the methods described above (and others) are used in both communities of faith and have often derived from methods of study originating in one or both of the communities. The special characteristics of Jewish and Christian readings will be explored in chapter 8. A discussion of the use of the Old Testament by the first Christian writers follows here.

The Old Testament in the New Testament

EXERCISE

📖 Read Acts 2:14–36. In Luke's account of one of the earliest Christian 'sermons', Peter is shown as quoting from the scriptures: Joel 2:28–32, Psalm 16:8–11, 132:11, 16:10 and 110:1.

How would you describe Peter's use of the Old Testament? What is he using it to do? Do the original contexts of the texts seem to be relevant to his purpose?

The characteristics of Jewish interpretation of scripture in the first century is found also among the first-century Christian-Jewish writings that now form the New Testament.

Jewish interpretation of scripture included a search for rules for living and this was centred on the texts of the Torah. Jesus in the Gospels is represented as answering questions about the Torah, and Paul uses the same methods as the rabbis in interpreting the Hebrew scriptures, in his focus on 'righteousness'.

However, in the lifetime of Jesus and the first Christian Jews, the Jewish sect of the Essenes tended to read biblical texts with a type of interpretation called 'pesher', as divine prophecies predicting the eschatological (end-time) conditions of their own community. This interpretation tended to centre on the prophetic literature rather than the Torah. This focus and method was very important in the central Christian affirmation of Jesus as the promised Messiah and the ideas of promise and fulfilment in the end-times brought about by God in Christ. Although the emphasis is prophecy rather than law, the prophetic voices included Moses (as the legendary author of the Pentateuch) and David (as the presumed author of all the Psalms) (Froehlich, 1993, p. 310).

The 'proof' from prophecy was very quickly the major tool of the first Christians in speaking to both Jews and Gentiles, in both mission and apologetics (defending their claims against opposition). Paul identifies the 'fulfilment of scripture' not only in the messiahship of Jesus but also in the nature of the end-times and events yet to be fulfilled, like the 'second coming' (Froehlich, 1993, p. 311).

Remember that the first Christians did not have the four Gospels or even one of them at first, but had only their first- or second- or third-hand experiences of Jesus' ministry, death and resurrection, and a developing oral tradition. The Hebrew scriptures were searched for clues about the significance of what had taken place among them, and the first method of biblical interpretation among them is overwhelmingly Christological. The way the Gospel writers tell their stories of Jesus is strongly influenced by these interpretations.

📖 **Read Matthew 2:13–15 and Hosea 11:1–5.** Matthew's interpretation of a phrase in Hosea is Christological. In the context in the Book of Hosea, 'my son' is not explicitly a messianic figure but refers to Israel, brought out of Egypt in the exodus, led by Moses. This may be an example of how an event in the life of Jesus (the flight into and return from Egypt, to which the other Gospels do not refer) is constructed out of a text in the Old Testament rather than interpreted by it. Matthew sees Jesus as a fulfilment of what is 'prefigured' in Moses, and so his life is seen as following the same pattern. Rather than an historical fact it is a theological truth – that Jesus is the child of God who leads and teaches God's people – that inspires the narrative. It is this theological truth that is informed by reflection on passages and ideas in the Old Testament.

📖 **Read Matthew 8:14–17 and Isaiah 53.** Reflection on the 'Suffering Servant' in parts of the Book of Isaiah seems to have been very important in early Christian reflection on the significance of Jesus.

EXERCISE

The verse cited by Matthew is Isaiah 53:4. Are there other parts of Isaiah 53 that the first (and later) Christians would read as messianic prophecy? Are there other signs of these ideas in the New Testament, as well as this one in Matthew 8?

Extraordinary texts

The familiarity of many readers with many parts of the Old Testament, and a tradition in the church of reading some parts and not others and of interpreting them with a particular perspective, may lead to a false sense of both what these books are about and how they can best be understood. It is the most extraordinary collection of texts. There is profound theology and human wisdom to be found in them, and there are coherent principles and developing themes. However, there are also deeply puzzling sayings, some distinctive ethics, and stories which defy a narrow perspective and a single method of interpretation. The inclusion of some books in the canon remains something of a mystery. Ecclesiastes is wonderful but not, on the face of it, very supportive of religious orthodoxy. In the Song of Songs, generations of scholars have sought in vain for some secret and unsexual meaning!

More factors are at work in the collection and interpretation of these texts than any one reader is likely to be able to compass. At the same time they are accessible texts, open for all sorts of readers to discover old wisdom or fresh insights.

📖 **Read Exodus 4:24–26.** This is a curious story, with some parallels to the story of Jacob wrestling in Genesis 32. What is a reader to make of this episode? The Almighty LORD appears to make an attempt on Moses' life, which is strange enough, but it is a failed attempt, which is odder still. Then a rather bizarre ritual seems to defeat or dissuade God.

The difficulty in interpreting it is not in the words; there is no real problem with the Hebrew here, nor are there significant manuscript variations. Translators inevitably interpret, and they have a choice about letting the reader face the difficulty or 'helping them out'. God's thwarted attempt at murder ('tried to kill') is not softened in the *New Revised Standard Version* and does seem to be what the Hebrew means. The *New International Version*'s 'was about to kill' and Knox's 'threatened to kill' seem designed to indicate that God's action was somehow provisional or feigned, which is still odd but suggests God had not intended to kill Moses in the first place.

EXERCISE
If you have access to a commentary on Exodus, look up what your commentator says about these verses. Does it shed any light?

Further reading

Old Testament introductions: histories and thematic surveys
Anderson, B (1988), *The Living World of the Old Testament* (fourth edition), London, Longman.
Rogerson, J and Davies, P (1990), *The Old Testament World*, Cambridge, Cambridge University Press.

Old Testament introductions: methodological
Barton, J (1984), *Reading the Old Testament: method in biblical study*, London, Darton, Longman and Todd.
Charpentier, E (1981), *How to Read the Old Testament*, London, SCM.
Coggins, R (1990), *Introducing the Old Testament*, Oxford, Oxford University Press.
Rogerson, J (1983), *Beginning Old Testament Study*, London, SPCK.

'Reading the gaps'
Exum, J C (1996), *Plotted, Shot, and Painted: cultural representations of biblical women*, Sheffield, Sheffield Academic Press.
Maitland, S (1993), *Daughter of Jerusalem*, London, Virago (the ends of each chapter).

The Old Testament in the New Testament
Bruce, F F (1978), *The Time is Fulfilled: five aspects of the fulfilment of the Old Testament in the New*, Carlisle, Paternoster.
Barr, J (1982), *Old and New Interpretation: a study of the two testaments*, London, SCM.

A good commentary on the whole Bible
Brown, R E, Fitzmyer, J A and Murphy, R E (eds) (1990), *The New Jerome Biblical Commentary*, London, Chapman.

4. READING THE NEW TESTAMENT

Introduction

This chapter considers the nature of the New Testament books and some of the key issues the reader has to deal with, including 'eschatology' and 'christology'. Two particular types of New Testament writing, Gospels and letters, will be discussed. We begin with points of comparison and contrast between these texts and the Old Testament texts considered in chapter 3.

Reflecting on experience

The experience of reading (or hearing) small passages of, say, the Gospels, in a church service, may be quite different from the experience of reading any one of the Gospels from beginning to end.

If you had read, say, a detective story, you would probably be able to tell someone else the basic plot or important episodes. Could you do that in just a few sentences, for any of the Gospels (choose one) without mixing in stories from one of the other Gospels? (If not, you could have a second stab at this after you have read Mark, a task later in this chapter.)

Contents and dates

The contents of the New Testament are 'canonically' ordered in this way:
- narratives of the ministry and passion of Jesus (the Gospels);
- narrative of what some of the disciples did next (*The Acts of the Apostles*);
- letters (though not all of them may have been exactly letters) to early

Christian communities from Paul and (mostly) second-generation
Christians (the old name 'epistles' means letters);
• book of apocalyptic prophecy (*Revelation*).

There is a logic to the ordering, which begins with accounts of
Jesus' ministry and Passion, continues with an account of the first
Jerusalem church and the mission of Paul, offers insights into the lives
of various Christian communities in letters that were written to them,
and finishes with a vision of the end-time. However, this does not
represent the order in which the books and letters were written.

There is a large degree of consensus on the dating of some books and
letters and not much consensus at all on others. Paul's letters probably
date from the late 40s to the early 60s. However, some of them bearing
his name might not be by him but by his followers, and these (perhaps
Ephesians) might be later by a decade or so, or as late as the 90s (1 and
2 Timothy and Titus). Some people put the letters of Jude and James
and the letter to the Hebrews in the 60s. The first gospel was probably
Mark and written just before or just after CE 70. Matthew, Luke, Revelation and 1 Peter (probably not by Peter himself) might all date from
the 80s. Acts might have been written in the 90s and John right at the
end of the century. The letters of John might be from the first decade of
the second century, and many scholars would put 2 Peter (and some
also Jude) in the second decade making this or these (perhaps) the
latest written texts included in the New Testament.

You will find a range of views on dating and authorship: a commentary on an individual book or letter will usually give you that scholar's
view on the matter.

Comparison and contrast with Old Testament books

It may be useful to think back to what we considered in chapter 3 about
the nature of the Old Testament books.

Like the Old Testament texts, the New Testament ones deal with God
and God's relationship with humanity and 'the people of God'; some
are set in the same territory of Israel and Judea, with a focus on
Jerusalem; they refer to the Torah and to the patriarchs and prophets
and early events like the exodus; they were/are used in 'lectionaries' and
are read out in public worship; they contain (elements of) prophecy,
poetry, proverbs, ethical codes, history, apocalyptic, parable, myth, etc.

Unlike the Old Testament texts, the New Testament ones were
(probably all) written in Greek, not Hebrew or Aramaic; they were

composed (and authored) within an 80-year period (late 40s to ?120s), not 1,000 years with a pre-history of oral composition and tradition; they are not much more than 25 per cent of the length of the Old Testament canon; and they have a tight thematic focus on the significance of Jesus.

Whereas Israel, the people of God, in the Old Testament might be defined by 'God, Land and Family' the people of God in the New Testament are defined by reference to Jesus the Christ. Different authors have different phrases to describe this: Paul writes of being 'in Christ', Mark of 'following' him, John of being one of Christ's 'own'.

The end-time

If three events may be seen as ones 'that existentially define Israel' as the people of God (Jacob wrestling, exodus, exile) are there three such which define the church in the New Testament as the people of God? We might suggest these as key:

- the death and resurrection of Jesus;
- the activity/presence of the Spirit of God;
- the end-time (*eschaton* in Greek: giving us the word 'eschatology', which means teaching about the end-time).

In fact these three (the Passion, the Spirit and the end-time) are all part of the *same* eschatological event. Resurrection and the outpouring of God's Spirit are features of the biblical understanding of what happens at the end-time.

This heightened focus on the end-time is a key difference between the Old and New Testaments. The time-scale of each is entirely different. The Old Testament (as a whole) has a view of 'salvation-history' from creation through to the fulfilment of God's promise (variously envisioned) of a blessing to the world through Abraham and his descendants. The New Testament texts describe not so much a history of salvation as a single 'salvation-event'.

This event, narratively, begins with the message of John the Baptist that a baptism of the Spirit was on its way. Jesus' ministry then proclaims or begins the reign of God, and Jesus' resurrection and the outpouring of the Spirit is the beginning of the end-time. The writers of the New Testament believe that they are those 'on whom the ends of the ages have come' (as Paul puts it in 1 Corinthians 10:11). They, and we in this eschatological view, live *between* the beginning-of-the-end (Jesus' resurrection) and the end-of-the-end (end of the world).

The scope of the Old Testament is huge: 'all human life is there'. The focus of the New Testament is much more specific. It is more overtly theological, more explicitly religious. There is very little in the New Testament that is not directly Christological (about the significance of Jesus) and/or directly eschatological (about the impact of the end-time).

The end-time is talked about in a number of ways but is always seen as the fulfilment of what has begun in Christ. Some of the teaching warns of the troubles and distress before the end-time comes; some of it encourages with a promise of fulfilment and the presence of God.

📖 **Read Mark 1:15.** This is Mark's summary of Jesus' proclamation: note the very 'eschatological' flavour of the message.

📖 **Read Mark 13:28–37.** This is part of a whole chapter of sayings of Jesus about the end-time. Here Jesus uses two images or parables to convey the ideas.

📖 **Read Acts 2:1–4 and 14–18.** Peter is shown as interpreting the outpouring of God's Spirit as the fulfilment of a promise about 'the last days'.

📖 **Read 1 Corinthians 15:20, 24 and 28.** Here Paul sees the end-time as beginning with the resurrection of Christ, including the destruction of all other powers and culminating in God who will be 'all in all'.

📖 **Read Revelation 21:1–4,** a vision of the end-time.

EXERCISE
The New Testament is full of language like this: through Jesus, God has brought about or is bringing about the end of all things. Drawing on the passages above, make a note of some of the ideas and words you are likely to come across when New Testament authors are writing about eschatology.

The Gospels

The Gospels are perhaps the most widely read of the texts in the New Testament, though probably far fewer people read one from beginning to end than hear or read small sections of them, like the bits that are read out in church services. There is also an understandable tendency to read one Gospel as if it were a quarter of a longer work called the Four Gospels, rather than a single authored text which stands on its own. The approach taken in this chapter will be to introduce a Gospel as a complete book which can be read independently of the rest of the New Testament.

Gospels are not easy to 'classify' as a type of ancient literature. In the Roman empire of the first century, there were different types of books written and copied. For example there were some called 'lives' (biography), 'acts' (deeds of the famous) and 'memoirs' (anecdotes of the famous by disciples or friends). The Gospels may have some characteristics of each of these but they may be distinct from any. For each of them the baptism of Jesus is a key starting point, and then there are sequences of stories about and sayings of Jesus which lead up to the longer narratives of his arrest, trial, crucifixion and resurrection.

The title they now have (they were not called 'the Gospel according to ...' by their first authors) is almost certainly an extension of Mark's use of the word in Mark 1:1: 'The beginning of the good news (Gospel) of Jesus Christ'. The Greek word translated as good news or Gospel is *euangelion* (giving us the word evangelist) and in the Roman empire referred to an act of proclamation, such as a military victory or the succession of an emperor. In Mark 1:1 it probably refers primarily to John the Baptist's proclamation, but the meaning was extended to refer to the literary form of the Gospel book.

The Gospels were probably intended to be read aloud in a congregation, not privately. They were probably read not in the short sections of today's church service readings, but in long sections or even the whole thing. The Gospels were designed for the ear rather than the eye, and this is reflected in the frequent repetitions and summaries. For example, three times Mark summarises Jesus' activity (1:32–34; 3:7–12; 6:56) which helps to convey the significance of the story as it is read (Hooker, 1993, p. 492).

EXERCISE

📖 **Read or re-read the Gospel of Mark.** Choose a modern translation (see the end of chapter 5 for notes on recommended modern translations). Try to read it at a single ▶▶

sitting (it is very short) to get a sense of the message and style of the whole book. Finish at 16:8 as some endings were added later.

If you had to describe what kind of a book or narrative the Gospel of Mark is, what would you say? Is it like a novel, a biography, a sermon, a drama or what?

Histories of Jesus?

Though there are the reports of eyewitnesses contained in the Gospels, none of the Gospels was written in the form we have it today by an eyewitness.

📖 **Read Luke 1:1–3.** One of the Gospels refers explicitly to its sources, and the stages that had preceded the Gospel. The author of the Gospel according to Luke says he has drawn on a number of written sources.

EXERCISE
What stages does Luke refer to as having taken place between the 'events' and his own 'orderly account?'

The Gospels are documents of their own times (Mark 60s/70s, Matthew and Luke 80s, John 90s) as well as documents about events in Jesus' times (30–33/34 CE). They are proclamations to their living communities, not (primarily) archives of past events. Each evangelist seems to have made a *selection* of the material available in the tradition in order to make their proclamation clear and effective. They presented the stories because they had a particular message to put across, and did it in a way intended to be *relevant* to their readership. Because they are writing to different communities in different times and places from one another, their messages and purposes (while sharing a great deal in common) are different.

EXERCISE
📖 **Read John 20:30–31.** It is clear from these verses that this ▶▶

writer is aware of a process of selection of the material available, and 20:31 states a particular intention behind the writing.

Mark has not told us in the same way why his Gospel was written. Can you speculate, from your reading of Mark's Gospel, what he might have written if at the end of his Gospel (at 16:8) he had chosen to make an explicit comment like John 20:31? Might it have been exactly the same or characteristically different? 'These things are written so that ...'

Selection and direction in a Gospel

The choice of which stories to include and the order to put them in were not therefore necessarily fixed by the order in which the events may have happened. Each Gospel writer has made choices about what to say and how to say it. Each of the Gospel writers has composed a very accomplished book, with remarkable narrative skills. (Literary questions will also be considered in chapter 7.)

EXERCISE

📖 **Remember your reading of Mark's Gospel.** Think of it as a whole narrative.

Note examples where the author has shaped the material, has grouped related episodes together, or developed a climax in the narrative. Do this before reading further: you may find other patterns than the examples chosen below.

In each of the Gospels, of course, the events around the arrest, trial and death of Jesus form a major, structured sequence. There are also frequent 'anticipations' and pointers to the Passion in the preceding chapters: one scholar even suggested that Mark is 'a Passion narrative with an extended introduction'.

Mark has divided Jesus' ministry geographically: the first ten chapters are set in Galilee, and then chapters 11 to 16 are set in Judea and Jerusalem.

There is a sequence of stories early on (Mark 2:1 to 3:6) where Jesus is shown meeting opposition. In 3:6 (very early in the whole book) Mark indicates how this opposition is going to culminate in Jesus being put to death.

There are two stories of Jesus healing blind men (8:22–26 and 10:46–52). The material in between seems to focus on the predicted suffering and death of Jesus and the response of the disciples. Are the two stories meant to act as a 'frame' to this collection of sayings? Is the metaphor of the blind seeing meant to apply to the growing perception (or lack of perception) of the disciples? Note how the second blind man becomes a follower of Jesus (10:52).

There is a characteristic arrangement of pairs of stories that is sometimes called a 'Markan sandwich'. This is where Mark starts telling one story, interrupts it to tell another, and then goes back to end the first story. It may be a dramatic device to keep the reader waiting for the resolution of the first story. It may have been his intention to let one of the stories impact on the reader's understanding of the other one: their significance may be connected. It is a sophisticated story-telling strategy.

EXERCISE

📖 **Read Mark 5:21–43 and 11:12–24.** These are examples of the 'Markan sandwich'.

Choose one of these examples. What links can you make between the two stories? What is the effect on the reader of hearing two stories sandwiched like this?

Mark's Christology

I suggested above, 'There is very little in the New Testament that is not directly Christological (about the significance of Jesus) and/or directly eschatological (about the impact of the end-time).' You have seen how eschatology is expressed in a number of ways but within a consistent framework. What about New Testament Christology?

As with eschatology, there is a wide variety of expression but a central core of ideas held in common. The titles Christ (or Messiah: God's Anointed), Son of God, Lord, are used about Jesus (and Son of Man *by* Jesus) in many different New Testament books. However, a fully formed, formally agreed analysis of the person and significance of Jesus was not available to the first generations of Christians. The later church debated and agreed its credal statements (for example, 'We believe in one Lord Jesus Christ ... true God, begotten not made, being of one substance with the Father') much later. The first Christians had to try to make sense of the significance of Jesus without the benefit of these fourth- and fifth-century formulas. Their pool of resources included Jesus' teaching and actions, the ideas in Judaism at the time about God's Messiah, the Hebrew scriptures and the *wholly unexpected element* of the crucifixion (and resurrection) of the Messiah.

In Romans 1:3–4, Paul may be quoting an early Christological statement used about Jesus in the first Palestinian churches:

> descended from David according to the flesh,
> and ... declared to be Son of God with power according to the spirit of holiness by resurrection from the dead.

Each author has characteristic ways of describing or indicating the significance of Jesus, as well as using phrases like these that perhaps many churches used.

EXERCISE

📖 **Re-read Mark; 1:21–28; 10:41–45; 15:33–39.**

What picture of Jesus do these episodes convey?

Are there other sections in Mark where, perhaps paradoxically, both *authority* and *humility* seem to be key to the understanding of Jesus?

If you know any of the other Gospels, do you think they have exactly the same emphasis? (For example, only Matthew includes that same cry of forsakenness on the cross.)

Paul's letters

Although the Gospels record incidents that happened in the ministry of Jesus, they were written several decades after the events. The earliest surviving Christian writings we have are Paul's letters, written ten or twenty years before the Gospel according to Mark.

Most or all of these really did start out as letters, written at a distance from the churches they were sent to, and directed to individuals and the gathered community of Christians in that place. How far Paul expected them to be copied and passed on to other churches in other places is not always clear. Some of them are evidently particular to the concerns of the people in just one place: they are 'occasional' in the sense of being a response to one particular occasion or set of circumstances. When Paul addresses a letter 'To all God's beloved in Rome' (Romans 1:7), were these Christians all gathered in the same house-church, or were there several separate gatherings of Christians in Rome? It is probably the latter, but we do not know.

Very early on in the history of the church, Paul's letters were known more widely than by the individual church to which any one letter was addressed. The author of 2 Peter (perhaps writing CE 110–120) refers to what Paul wrote, saying that he speaks about this 'as he does in all his letters' (2 Peter 3:16). This suggests a widespread use of a *body* of Paul's letters 50 or so years after his death. (It may or may not comfort you to learn that the author of 2 Peter did not find Paul easy reading! He says in the same verse, 'There are some things in them hard to understand ...')

EXERCISE

📖 **Read the letter of Paul to Philemon.** This is one of the shortest items in the Bible.

What seems to have been the 'occasion' that caused Paul to write this letter? (Verses 10, 16 and 17 might be key.)

It has not remained a personal letter asking for something; now it is in everyone's Bible! Why might it have been seen as more than of 'occasional' importance? Is it an example of something important to all Christians?

We will use this letter to illustrate some of the characteristics of Paul, his letters and his churches:

and (from) Timothy our brother ... (verse 1). It is probable that Paul's letters were usually dictated to one of his co-workers who wrote while Paul spoke. It is likely that for this letter Timothy was the 'amanuensis' or secretary, as Sosthenes is for 1 Corinthians (see 1 Corinthians 1:1). Would this writer contribute at all to the contents of the letter? It is hard to say. Sometimes Paul apparently took hold of the pen himself in order to make a personal gesture (see Philemon 19, and Galatians 6:11). In some portions of letters where Paul is making complex arguments, his sentences do not 'resolve' grammatically, and it may be that dictating, rather than writing and constantly reviewing what he had written, contributes to this. However, often Paul's prose is masterly in rhetoric and expression.

and to the church in your house (verse 2). The first Christians had no public or 'parish' buildings to meet in but gathered in someone's own house. Archaeology suggests that the biggest dining room of a wealthy person would be unlikely to be able to accommodate more than 40 or 50 people, so presumably if the church grew larger than this, they would have to be hosted by more than one household.

Even this personal letter is directed to the whole community and not just the three people named (perhaps all three are of the host household). Paul's manner (and theology) reflects an expectation of Christians sharing together in many aspects of life. In his famous 'grace' (2 Corinthians 13:13) the phrase 'the *fellowship of* the Holy Spirit' could be translated 'the *common life in* the Holy Spirit'.

When I remember you in my prayers ... I would rather appeal to you on the basis of love (verses 4 and 9). Paul is passionately committed to the people to whom he writes. These are, in a sense, love letters. Apart from the letter to the Romans, all the surviving letters are written to churches Paul has visited and probably founded. He knows these people, he has brought them to faith in Christ and thinks of himself, sometimes, as their father (for example, Philemon 10). They are letters of a pastor trying to maintain a pastoral role at a distance. The letter to the Romans may be different because he has not that same 'foundation' relationship (though he is at pains to make personal references to many of the congregation in chapter 16).

I am bold enough in Christ to command ... (verse 8). There is a persistent theme in Paul's letters (sometimes an undercurrent rather than something explicit) of the question of his authority. Two things are at stake. One is the independence of his authority from the leaders of the Jerusalem churches (read what he says about them in Galatians 2:6; these leaders included Peter and James the brother of Jesus). There were clearly those who denied his apostleship: 'If I am not an apostle to others, at least I am to you' (1 Corinthians 9:2). The other matter at stake is Paul's own theology, which was not based on command, rights and status, but on grace, freedom and love (demonstrated in the cross of Christ). It matters to him that Philemon should respond to his request freely out of love because that is how the Gospel works. The evangelist John has often been called 'the apostle of love' but, arguably, Paul has as much or more claim to the title.

I am sending him ... back to you (verse 12). There was no public mail service in the Empire: letters had to be carried by hand and someone had to make an expensive, and sometimes dangerous, journey to take a letter. The grain ships could be used for journeys by sea, and the Egnatian Way linked major cities in Asia Minor by land. It is worth remembering therefore that we do not have in the written letter the whole of the messages that passed on these occasions between Paul and his churches: someone brought the letter and could speak about Paul's views and give other information. On this occasion it is probably Onesimus himself who brings the letter and, surely, had views himself on what he wanted to happen!

Further reading

On reading the New Testament
Charpentier, E (1982), *How to Read the New Testament*, London, SCM.
Tuckett, C (1987), *Reading the New Testament*, London, SPCK.
Walton, R C (ed.) (1980), *A Basic Introduction to the New Testament*, London, SCM.
On the Gospel of Mark
Hooker, M D (1993), Mark, The Gospel according to, in B M Metzger and M D Coogan (eds), *The Oxford Companion to the Bible*, Oxford, Oxford University Press.
Hooker, M D (1981), *The Message of Mark*, London, Epworth.
On Paul
Ziesler, J (1990), *Pauline Christianity* (revised edition), Oxford, Oxford University Press.
On eschatology, Christology, Gospel, Paul, Mark
Metzger, B M and Coogan, M D (eds) (1993), *The Oxford Companion to the Bible*, Oxford, Oxford University Press.
Brown, R E, Fitzmyer, J A and Murphy, R E (eds) (1990), *The New Jerome Biblical Commentary*, London, Chapman.
Green, J B, McKnight, S and Marshall, I H (eds) (1992), *Dictionary of Jesus and the Gospels*, Leicester, IVP.

5. USING WORDS: METAPHOR AND TRANSLATION

Introduction

Using the Bible means using words about God and God's relationship with humanity. This chapter looks at two key concerns to do with the words in the Bible, and reading them with understanding. It will ask, 'How are words and names used to talk about an indescribable and ineffable (un-nameable) God?' and 'How does the act of the translation of words affect the meaning of what we read?'

> **Reflecting on experience**
> Some people's minds are more 'visual' than others: if you are asked to think about 'God' or 'heaven' or 'the Holy Spirit', do you think of words and ideas associated with them or visualise pictures of them?
>
> Choose one (God, heaven, Spirit): what words or what pictures come to mind? Do any of them seem to you accurate and adequate?

God-talk and metaphor

In religious language, it is often the case that we only have a picture language to indicate what we mean: talk about God and spiritual things has to use language 'borrowed' from the human and physical world. So biblical authors may call God 'Father', or Jesus 'Light of the World', or use for the Spirit of God the same word they use for 'breath' and 'wind'.

These 'borrowed images' are all the words (or signs) we have, apart perhaps from some abstract philosophical terms like 'omniscient' (all-knowing) or 'intangible' (untouchable, not physical), to talk about spiritual experience and spiritual reality, to express what is otherwise inexpressible. Religious discourse is full of metaphor, simile, analogy and other ways of perceiving similarity and likeness. Jesus was a very able user of metaphorical language, with sayings like 'The Kingdom of God is like a mustard seed ...' This parable uses a simile ('is like') for expressing the similarity between a spiritual idea and a tangible thing; and the 'Kingdom' is itself a metaphor, God's sovereignty or authority being pictured as the reign of a monarch.

If you have ever seen a signer at work in a service of worship, translating the spoken and sung liturgy into sign language for the deaf, you will have observed someone taking biblical words and turning them into physical signs. A lot of the signs use elements of mime and imitation, a picture language. This illustrates what spoken or written words are often doing too: offering a picture or story to name or describe something.

EXERCISE

Consider these lines from a well-known Wesleyan hymn:

> Long my imprisoned spirit lay, fast bound in sin and nature's night;
> Thine eye diffused a quickening ray – I woke, the dungeon flamed with light,
> My chains fell off, my heart was free, I rose, went forth and followed thee.

What is the nature of the experience that is being described? What picture language is being used to describe it? Why was it chosen?

📖 **Read Acts 12:6–10.** There may be a general idea but also a specific biblical story behind an image. How far does this passage give a context for the metaphor that helps us to understand the meaning?

Signers, like translators (or hymn writers), have to make conscious decisions all the time about what metaphor they are going to use. If a signer needs to sign 'salvation' or 'to save', the signer might need to know the church tradition of the congregation or the speaker, because 'save' can be expressed in a number of ways. One is a gesture where one hand appears to gather things in towards the body and this gesture can also be used to mean 'harvest'. Another mimics the placing of a coin in the palm of the hand, the payment of a price. Each of these images has a place among many metaphors and analogies used in the Bible to describe what God achieves in Christ for humanity. Different church traditions tend to emphasise different ones. The collectivism of the 'gathering' image will probably strike a particular chord with Catholic congregations; the 'payment of a price' metaphor is the primary idea in atonement doctrine for some Protestant traditions. The biblical authors often use several different images to express something like this, which is difficult to express.

Users of the Bible are perhaps often not conscious of when they are using the metaphors or from what situation they have been 'borrowed'. This is the case with more than just religious language: often we forget in daily speech that we are using a metaphor. Most of us, most of the time, surely forget when we lift the flat 'bonnet' of a modern car, that on old cars the structure covering the engine used to look rather like an old fashioned hat, and so got its name.

Translators of the Bible have the choice of keeping a metaphor from the Hebrew or Greek which they translate into comparable terms in the new language. However, what if the metaphor does not make any sense in the new language? There is an anecdote of translators of the Bible encountering the language of an inland, tent-dwelling people who had no word for 'anchor'. When they got to Hebrews 6:19, 'We have this hope, a sure and steadfast anchor of the soul ...', they translated 'anchor' as 'tent-peg', which had meaning to the speakers of that language. Is this a faithful translation, faithful to the meaning if not to the words of the Bible?

IT DEPENDS ...

There is a long-standing series of jokes about how many people of different sorts it takes to change a light bulb. One, relevant for this discussion of religious language, is:

Q 'How many liberal Christians does it take to change a light bulb?'
A 'Well, it depends what you mean by "light bulb" ...'

The liberals (whatever is meant by that, because 'it depends what you mean by "liberal"') have got it right here: in religious talk ▶▶

> and writing, including the biblical texts, our understanding has to include, 'It depends what you mean by "anchor", or "save" or "Kingdom".'

When people talk about religious matters, and use the language of the Bible, they are using metaphors. This does not mean that they believe that the inexpressible things are not real or that the God who cannot be seen, touched or named, does not exist and cannot be encountered. Rather, they are accepting that this language can be used to describe things which cannot be touched or seen. Indeed the author of Hebrews describes faith as 'the certainty of things not seen'. Whether God is real or not is a matter of faith; the language about it is religious discourse which we have to use to speak about the ideas, whatever our beliefs.

However, people do not always acknowledge this and over-literal thinking can lead to a breakdown of meaning among users of the Bible. We might make a claim for the meaningfulness of the phrase 'the Lamb of God, who takes away the sin of the world' (John 1:29). However, if we are assumed to be describing something literally, perhaps 'a sheep with a wheelbarrow', the meaning is of course emptied or distorted beyond recognition.

EXERCISE

Consider these metaphors. The following phrases are drawn from biblical passages:
- The LORD is my rock.
- The LORD is my shepherd.
- Jesus is the Lamb of God.
- God is our Judge.
- Our Father who art in heaven.
- Jesus is the Son of God.

How far could any of these be claimed to be *literally* true? How far does any depend on a particular context to make sense?

The LORD is my rock. There may be a particular historical context for this image in Psalm 18. The basic idea of security, firmness, permanence is apparent, but this psalm is headed by a note about its composition by

David, and the rock in the mind of the author might be the hill fortress of Masada.

The LORD is my shepherd. The image in Psalm 23 is extended to describe God in terms of the shepherd's job of leading, feeding, comforting. 'Lord' is also a metaphor of course. A lord is literally a male human who has a cultural or military leadership role. The metaphor says that God is *like this* in some way. (The word in the Hebrew text translated here as 'LORD' is actually 'YHWH', the name of God. We do not know for certain how this was pronounced and the Jews by tradition do not pronounce it but substitute a word for 'Lord' as Christian Bibles mostly do too. Your Bible will usually acknowledge that it is not the word in the text by writing LORD in capital letters.)

Jesus is the Lamb of God. The reference seems to rely on the very particular context of the cultic sacrifice of animals at the Jerusalem Temple, though the phrase 'takes away the sin of the world' (John 1:29) makes it seem more like the scapegoat (Leviticus 16:8).

God is our Judge. If we believe that God will judge humanity, this one might be said, within our faith, to be literally true. In some passages however, the context of the Judges like Deborah and Gideon, the military and civil rulers of Israel before the time of the kings, might be more in the mind of the biblical author. God for the author(s) is like or acts like those women and men.

Our Father who art in heaven. Literally speaking, fatherhood is biological, to do with male animals and male humans. If God is not physical and not gendered, God cannot literally be a father. This is one of those metaphors (like the bonnet of a car) that is so embedded in language and religious life that it is hard for many of us to see it as 'only' a metaphor. 'Who art in heaven' is a phrase characteristic of Matthew, and Luke's version of the prayer does not have it. The heavens or the skies are a designation for the location of God, in the double-decker view of the cosmos, the world below and God above, which the Bible often uses. 'Our heavenly Father', or even 'God our Father' probably gives the meaning.

Jesus is the Son of God. See the note above on 'Father' for the biological literalism of the parent/child metaphor. Clearly the two sentences that follow mean fundamentally different things:

Jesus	is	the Son of	God.
Jason Connery	is	the son of	Sean Connery.

Nevertheless, there is something in the relationship of a human father and son that makes this language meaningful when used of God and Jesus. There may be many similarities. Is it that an obedient child does what the parent desires? Or is it that sons often do what their fathers do (and Jesus loves, judges, saves, like God)? There may be a more specific context that this idea is using also, because the phrase 'son of God' has a range of uses in the Old Testament. There it is used of righteous people beloved by God or particular individuals chosen by God, like a prophet, or the king. Some of these things may be part of the context needed to understand what the New Testament means by the term.

The un-nameable God

There are some regular pious circumlocutions (roundabout ways of speaking which evade a difficult issue). Some of the metaphors and images reflect a particular Jewish concern with the proper respect due to God and the commandment, 'You shall not make wrongful use of the name of the LORD your God' (Exodus 20:7). The regular, pious, substitution of 'LORD' for 'YHWH' has already been noted.

EXERCISE

📖 Compare Matthew 3:2 with Mark 1:15.

In what way is Matthew more cautious or more pious than Mark in the words he is prepared to use?

📖 Read Luke 15:7 and 10.

What phrase does Luke use rather than write: 'God rejoices'?

Words not pictures

Sometimes, as in some of the examples in the exercise above, there are particular historical or cultural matters that help the reader to understand what the meaning of a word or phrase or image may be. It may be helpful to know, for example, that a lot of Hebrew imagery is not visual, in the sense of 'being envisaged' by the author.

📖 **Read Revelation 5:5–6.** In verse 5, the same thing is both a Lion and a Root. In verse 6 there is a Lamb 'standing as if it had been slaughtered'. These are hard to imagine visually, though Christian artists have attempted to paint the slain Lamb.

📖 **Read Revelation 21:2.** The image has a descending city that is also like an adorned bride. This is a 'mixed metaphor' where the symbolism of each part is meaningful, but they are not part of the same 'picture'.

In these instances it seems as if the author is more concerned about *significance* than *appearance*; the reader is not meant to ask 'What would that look like?' but rather 'What does that mean?' The importance given to significance rather than appearance may well be connected to the prohibition on 'carved images' in the Ten Commandments in Jewish law.

New Testament metaphors of salvation

This section is concerned with the language used in the New Testament to talk about the plight of humanity and the resolution of this in Jesus.

We looked at two examples of how a signer might interpret the word 'save' in a Christian context. The exercise that follows looks at the images biblical authors used in their words about God saving humanity. 'Salvation' meaning 'liberation' is itself only one of the metaphors used about what God does: the Christian tradition refers to the issue as the doctrine of atonement. The New Testament writers use many images to speak of the 'alienation' of humanity from God, and many corresponding images of how God in Christ 'mends' or 'heals' (these are yet more metaphors) the situation.

EXERCISE

📖 **Look up Mark 10:45b; 2 Corinthians 5:20; 1 Corinthians 15:24–25; Hebrews 10:11–12; Romans 5:18; Romans 8:22–23.**

In each of the passages, you are looking for:

- the *problem*: what image is given or implied about the plight of humanity that needs a solution?
- the *answer* to the problem: what corresponding image is given or implied of what Jesus does, or what God does in Jesus?
- the *(social) context* of the metaphor or simile: what is the background idea or picture which helps to make sense of the words used?

Take Mark 10:45b for an example. Sometimes it is easier to start with the statement about the solution and work back to the idea of the problem it solves:
- the solution: a ransom
- the problem: captivity or slavery
- the context of the metaphor: slavery, where slaves could be ransomed by the payment of a price.

Translation and interpretation: a case study

This section uses the Lord's Prayer, in Luke and Matthew and in various prayer book versions, to illustrate the kinds of interpretative decisions that have gone into any translation of a biblical passage. Any translation involves decisions of interpretation, and these decisions can be influenced by many things: by other versions of the same or of a similar text, by traditions and old words made familiar with use, by particular religious beliefs, by consciousness of words changing their meanings from one culture to another or over time, by the purpose of the translation (study, worship, poetry, inclusiveness, accessibility) and by many other factors.

The prayer that Christians refer to as 'the Lord's Prayer' derives from versions of a model of praying given by Jesus to his disciples in two of the Gospels. Not many Christians use the Greek of the manuscripts of these Gospels (not even in Greece as modern Greek is not the same as the Greek of 2,000 years ago). Jesus almost certainly spoke Aramaic rather than Greek, so the manuscripts are already a translation of a Semitic language. (We do know the Aramaic word that Jesus used for 'Father', which was 'Abba': see Mark 14:36.)

Remember that the Gospels, written in Greek, translate sayings of

Jesus made in Aramaic. These Aramaic versions were either unrecorded or have been lost.

Note first that the two Gospels do not record the same form of words, so there are, from the furthest back we can get, already two different versions. (The *New Revised Standard Version* is fairly 'literal' but is still influenced by traditions of interpretation, like using the old word 'hallowed'.)

Luke 11:2–4 New Revised Standard Version, 1989	*Matt 6:9–13 New Revised Standard Version, 1989*
Father, hallowed be your name.	Our Father in heaven, hallowed be your name.
Your kingdom come.	Your kingdom come. Your will be done, on earth as it is in heaven.
Give us each day our daily bread.*	Give us this day our daily bread.
And forgive us our sins, for we ourselves forgive everyone indebted to us.	And forgive us our debts, as we also have forgiven our debtors.
And do not bring us to the time of trial.	And do not bring us to the time of trial, but rescue us from the evil one.*
*or our bread for tomorrow.	*or from evil. Some manuscripts add (in varying forms) for the kingdom and the power and the glory are yours forever. Amen.

Compare these. Matthew's is longer, mostly because of 'doublet' phrases, which are near repetitions of a phrase by another with a similar meaning. This is like a feature of Hebrew poetry called 'parallelism'. Either Jesus or Matthew, each familiar with scriptural texts that use parallelism, might have done this. But why would Luke have left them out? Do we have two different occasions and two different prayers, or is one a development, expansion or contraction, of the other?

Here is the Greek version in Matthew constructed from some of the best manuscripts with an approximate English translation, word for word, beneath:

Matthew 6:9–13 Greek, c. CE 85
(from manuscripts second
to fifth centuries)

Pater hēmōn ho   en tois ouranois, hagiasthētō to onoma sou,
Father our the(one)in the heavens; Let it be holy the name of you (sing.);

elthetō   hē basileia sou,   genēthētō to thelēma   sou,   hōs en
let it come the kingdom of you; let it happen the will/desire of you as   in
ouranō kai epi gēs.

heaven also on earth;
Ton arton hēmōn ton epiousion   dos hēmin sēmeron,
the bread of us   (the) of today/tomorrow   give to us   today;
kai aphes hēmin ta opheilēmata hēmōn,
and cancel (for) us the debts   of us
hōs kai hēmeis aphēkamen tois opheiletais hēmōn,
as   also we   have let off   the   debtors   of us;
kai mē eisenegkēs hēmas eis peirasmon, alla hrusai hēmas apo tou
and not bring   us   into time of trial but   rescue us   from
ponērou.
(the) evil.

The Latin translation used in the western church from the fourth
century to the present day has often influenced subsequent versions.
Older versions (like this) did not have access to the full range of manuscripts or linguistic knowledge that later versions do:

Matt 6:9–13 The Vulgate c. CE 384–1590

Pater noster, qui es in cœlis: santificetur   nomen tuum.
Father our   who is in heavens: made holy be name   your.
Adveniat   regnum tuum. Fiat voluntas tua, sicut in cœlo,   et
May it come reign   your. Be will/desire your as   in heaven also
in terra.
on earth
Panem nostrum supersubstantialem   da nobis hodie.
Bread our   necessary-to-support-life give to us   today.
Et   dimitte nobis debita nostra,
And dismiss from us debts   our
sicut et   nos dimittimus debitoribus nostris.
as   also we dismiss   debtors   our
Et   ne nos inducas in   tentationem. sed libera nos a   malo.
and not us   lead   into temptation but free   us   from evil.

The use of the prayer in Christian worship in English has a distinc-
tive tradition of translation which derives partly from the Latin version.
The versions most people know are not exactly that of either Luke or
Matthew, but a church conflation. Patterns of phrases recur from one

version to another. *The Alternative Service Book 1980* of the Church of England closely follows *The Book of Common Prayer* 1662 version, as the pattern and meaning that Anglicans were used to. In these ways, several well-known versions are not exactly translating a biblical text.

Other translations have been differently motivated: some (for example Morley's below) have gone back to the Greek text afresh, usually Matthew. In several versions (for example Morley's and Furlong's) alternative translations have been found for gendered words, like 'Kingdom' and 'Father', and the 'desire' or longing rather than the 'will' or command of God has been emphasised.

EXERCISE

Highlight significant differences between the three modern versions below, and consider possible reasons for the translators having chosen one word or phrase rather than another. Does the Greek text give them the ideas expressed, or are they following a tradition of interpretation, or is there a new element in a new version?

If you have a preference for one translation over another, state reasons for your preference.

Alternative Service Book 1980
Our Father in heaven,
hallowed be your name;
your kingdom come, your will be done on earth as in heaven;
give us today our daily bread;
forgive us our sins, as we forgive those who sin against us;
lead us not into temptation,
but deliver us from evil;
for the kingdom, the power and the glory are yours, now and forever.

Matt 6:9–13, Janet Morley 1988
Abba our God,
whom the heavens disclose,
may your name be held holy,
your authority come.
May your longing be fulfilled
as in heaven, so on earth.

Give us today the bread of tomorrow,
and cancel our debts
as we have already forgiven our debtors.
Do not draw us in to sinful enticement,
but set us free from the grip of evil;
for authority and power and glory
are yours alone, for ever.

The Prayer of Jesus, Monica Furlong 1980s

God, who cares for us,
The wonder of whose presence fills us with awe,
Let kindness, justice and love shine in our world.
Let your secrets be known here as they are in heaven.
Give us the food and the hope we need for today.
Forgive us our wrongdoing
as we forgive the wrongs done to us.
Protect us from pride and despair
and from fear and hate which can swallow us up.
In you is truth, meaning, glory and power,
while worlds come and go*. Amen.

*In the Latin tradition, 'for ever' was translated *in saecula saeculorum* which is
literally 'in the worlds of worlds' or 'in the ages of ages'.

Further reading

Achtemeier, E (1993), Metaphors, in B Metzger and M D Coogan (eds), *The
   Oxford Companion to the Bible*, Oxford, Oxford University Press.
Barton, J and Balentine, S E (eds) (1994), *Language, Theology and the Bible*,
   Oxford, Oxford University Press.
Caird, G B (1980), *The Language and Imagery of the Bible*, London, Duckworth.
Metzger, B M (1989), To the reader, a preface to *Holy Bible, New Revised Standard
   Version*, Oxford, Oxford University Press.

6. USING HISTORICAL SKILLS

Introduction

Christianity is a religion founded in history. It springs from the traditions and beliefs of Judaism, which is characterised by a 'salvation-history' of God's relationship with the world. It hinges on historical events around the historical person of Jesus of Nazareth. It uses the historical tradition of the subsequent church as part of its authority and identity.

Some historical questions have already begun to be raised in this book. In chapter 2 we saw how the Bible has been interpreted through history. In chapters 3 and 4 we saw how the books of the Old Testament and the books and letters of the New Testament can be read with attention to their historical situation.

This chapter focuses on the historical-critical tradition as a way of understanding and using the Bible. Particular questions of 'historicity' (historical value and validity), especially some relating to the ministry of Jesus, will be examined.

Reflecting on experience
Consider an historical event – anything from world history or from your family history which took place before you were born.

What are the sources of your information (letter, newspaper, oral report, school book, school teacher ...)? Can you test any of your sources against others that record the same or different facts? Did any of your sources give the story a 'spin' or bias, or was it all 'accurate reporting'? Can you be sure?

Historical books in the Bible

There are books in the Bible which appear to have an interest in history. Some categorisations of the Old Testament refer to some of them as the 'historical books' (for example, Samuel, Kings, Chronicles). Chronicles has a name which suggests a deliberate intention to 'chronicle' historical events. In the New Testament, the Book of Acts, in a way, chronicles the history of the early church from the birth of the Jerusalem church at Pentecost to Paul's arrival in Rome, the capital of the empire.

Nevertheless, these are not historical books in the modern sense, if by 'history' we understand an analysis of sources and a sifting of evidence in order to establish the most plausible and reliable reconstruction of past events. The biblical authors and editors are writing for purposes that are likely to transcend the purely historical. They are selective, interpretative and have a message about the revelation of God in the lives of the 'people of God'. This is not to say that they set out to distort the past, nor to deny that they provide a wide range of material that the modern historian can use. The records, though, have been set down not to record the events of the reigns of kings and the policies of nations but to reveal and proclaim the purposes of God. They are books of faith before they are books of history.

This is also true of the Gospels: their intention is not historical biography but proclamation of the good news.

The Gospels and historical thinking

Our focus for issues of the Bible and history will be the Gospels. These are by no means the only issues or books we could look at, but some of the historical issues are of key importance for how the Bible is read and used.

It is important to note that history only deals with some types of human enquiry and some types of evidence. In the same way that you would not expect a class in geometry, looking at pyramids, to discuss the lives and beliefs of the Pharaohs of Egypt, nor expect an article on astronomy, examining 'black holes', to spend time discussing the poetry of despair, so there are subjects of human interest that history does not cover. History is not theology nor philosophy nor poetry, and does not explain nor seek to explain the origin of the universe, the activity of the Holy Spirit or the divine mystery of love. Individual historians may or may not have a view on these things, but they are not dealing with them when they are doing history.

For example, consider how we might discuss the death and resurrection of Jesus. First, consider the crucifixion:

Jesus died for the salvation of the world	*Jesus of Nazareth was crucified*
This is a statement of faith, not open to historical investigation.	This is a well-attested historical fact. It is open to the same kind of investigation from the same type of sources as, say, 'Nelson died at the Battle of Trafalgar'.

Then consider the resurrection:

God raised Jesus from death	*The followers of Jesus within a short time of Jesus' death behaved as if they were convinced that he had been raised by God.*
This is a statement of faith, neither verifiable nor falsifiable by historians.	This much is a matter of historical record. Whether his followers believed it because it was true, or believed it because they were deluded, or whether they lied, it is not possible to demonstrate by historical means.

The 'quest for the historical Jesus'

Almost all our evidence for the details of the life and ministry of Jesus and for the actions of the disciples after his death comes from texts written by the first- and second-generation Christians. The Gospel writers wrote *after* the resurrection about things that had happened *before* the resurrection. It is likely to the point of certainty that what they came to believe about Jesus after his death will have made an impact on what they wrote about his life. Indeed they would surely not have written about his life at all if they were not proclaiming him as the one whom God had raised. Did this belief and proclamation colour their accounts? Did it distort them? Did they even *intend* to give an historical portrait of Jesus, or was their intention rather to help their readers to an understanding of his (beyond-historical) significance? Was the actual 'Jesus of history' not entirely like the person they described who is really the 'Christ of faith'? This was one of the great post-Enlightenment debates

which has had a lasting effect in a number of ways. There is on the whole agreement among scholars today on the following:
- The Gospels are indeed concerned with proclamation and are indeed written with the perspective of a post-Easter faith.
- The post-resurrection faith of the first Christians is nevertheless *not* wholly divorced from the ministry of Jesus that went before it: there is continuity as well as difference in the history of Jesus of Nazareth and the proclamation of faith about him.
- Certain 'tools' of criticism can be used to try to decide whether the material about Jesus has been given an unhistorical treatment.

The 'archaeology' of Gospel texts

We could picture the text of the Gospels as being like the site of an archaeological dig. On a dig, for example in a city like Chester, beneath the surface of today's world may be finds from a nineteenth-century layer; and beneath that is the medieval layer waiting to be unearthed, and beneath that again, the Roman city. It depends what layer you want to reach whether you use a fine brush, a trowel, a spade or, drastically, a bulldozer. In the text of the Gospel, we can use different tools depending on which layer of history we are trying to get at. There have been trends or fashions in the tools that can be used on the biblical texts, often responding to the successes and failures of the tools and trends that previous scholars used.

'Layers' of Gospel text	Tools used
The text and the reader today	Literary criticism
The situation and intention of the author/evangelist	Redaction criticism; social history;
The time between the actions narrated and the finished Gospel(s)	Form criticism (and tradition criticism)
The life and ministry of Jesus, c. 30–33 CE	Criterion of difference; criterion of plausibility; social history; source criticism

If we are trying to examine the top layer, the text and the reader today, we need first of all the reading skills by which we make sense of character, plot, and dialogue. This is a type of criticism which need not interest itself in historical questions (read further in chapter 7). We may be reading a Gospel as a story which, whatever it has been in the past, is now a story with a meaning and application in today's world. The characters are people like ourselves or types known to us. They say and do things which demonstrate thoughts and feelings to which we relate. It would not matter if the text had been written yesterday, there is meaning in it.

If we are interested historically in the world of the author (here the author of one of the Gospels) we can look for the meaning of the text as it may have been intended by the author (though we may not know who the author was) who wrote the text for particular readers or hearers in a particular time and place. Redaction criticism and socio-historical approaches are each discussed below.

Beneath, or before, the time of the evangelist is the 30 and more years of the earliest Christian communities. With form criticism (also 'tradition criticism' – see below) we can look at the different 'units of tradition' of which the Gospels are composed (parables, healing miracles, sayings of Jesus, short stories, etc.) and try to work out what they meant in the earliest Christian communities, in the times when they were created and passed on orally.

The earliest historical period in the Gospels, the 'bottom layer' of our archaeological dig, is the period of Jesus' historical ministry. With a number of tools (some have been tried and rejected as not reliable) we can try to analyse the likely historical events that took place. The event lie behind or beneath the stories passed on in the oral tradition. Those oral stories in turn lie behind the texts of the Evangelists.

We will look at some of them, not in the historical sequence in which they were developed but with reference to these layers of history that might lie within our texts. We will mostly work upwards through the layers starting with the textual tools that try to unearth the history of Jesus.

Difference, plausibility and social history

A subsequent development to the failure of the nineteenth-century 'quest' of the historical Jesus was a new method used to find the historically authentic Jesus (it developed among Rudolph Bultmann's pupils). It is a *criterion of difference*, sometimes referred to as the 'double-dissimilarity' criterion. What you have to do is to exclude as historically doubtful anything in the Gospels that could be derived directly from Judaism or from the early (post-Easter) church. If it could have been derived from either of these (the theory goes) we cannot be sure that the Gospel writers got a particular teaching or idea from Jesus.

📖 **Read Mark 9:1 and John 1:51.** In each of these verses (and in many others) Jesus starts a saying with 'Truly'. In the Greek manuscripts, this is given as the Hebrew word 'Amen'. Did Jesus really characteristically say this, or is it a post-Easter interpretation? Let us apply the criterion of difference.

first-century Judaism	*the historical Jesus*	*the early church*
Jews used 'Amen' (for example Numbers 5:22) in agreement and response, particularly to prayer, rather as evangelical Christian congregations do. There are few, if any, examples of Jews other than Jesus using 'Amen' as a preface to a statement.	'Amen, I say to you …'	No one else in the New Testament texts uses 'Amen' as preface in this way: it does not seem to have been a use of the post-Easter church which is 'read back' into the time of Jesus. 'Amen' is used, as in Judaism, in response to prayer and prophecy, for example Revelation 22:20–21.

Jesus' use seems to be distinctive and it is therefore extremely likely to be an authentic tradition that the historical Jesus sometimes prefaced solemn statements with 'Amen'. This does not mean that *all* the statements prefaced with this in the Gospels are as certainly authentic: the Evangelists may have multiplied this characteristic of the historical Jesus.

The odd thing about this method, of course, is that it appears to demand a separation of Jesus, a Jew, from the Judaism of his time, and also to use a premiss that nothing that Jesus used in his proclamation was used by the first Christians in their own proclamation, which would mean they got it *all* wrong! In fact this method was used by many only as a first stage, to identify a critically certain minimum of authentic Jesus tradition. A critic can then consider how coherent other traditions are with this historically secure minimum (Theissen and Merz, 1998, p. 92).

However, the scholars who today research into the historical issues about Jesus are more likely to use a *criterion of plausibility* than a *criterion of difference* (Theissen and Merz, 1998, p. 10). They too look across on one side to Judaism and on the other to the early church, but they ask, 'Is this action or saying of Jesus plausible in the context of first-century Judaism?' and 'Does it make the later development of early Christianity understandable?'

There are two key elements to this later methodology (Theissen and Merz, 1988). There is an interest in the place of Jesus in Judaism. Modern historical-critical scholarship tends to take more seriously than before the fundamentally Jewish nature both of the proclamation of Jesus and of the origins of the early church. There is also an interest in social history. By studying comparable, contemporary social situations, like the tensions in Jewish society at the time of Jesus and renewal movements with prophetic leaders in other cultures, scholars can more accurately judge what is historically plausible. They also research the social continuity between the pre-Easter disciples and the post-Easter church: for example, the earliest travelling preachers of Christianity seem to have continued the preaching and lifestyle of Jesus.

Using source criticism for historical investigation

The aim of source criticism of the Gospels was to find the earliest written version of the traditions about Jesus, and this was done largely in the hope of establishing the events that lay behind them: the history of Jesus. In fact of course even the earliest version of an event is still an *interpretation* of it. You could ask two people today about what they did together yesterday and you might get two versions with a different perspective, a different 'spin' to the story. So with source criticism the historical events (and particularly the historical Jesus) can still prove elusive.

📖 **Revisit Luke 1:1–3 and the exercise in chapter 4.** This Evangelist has several characteristics of an historian: for example, see his phrase, 'after investigating everything carefully' (1:3).

One of the biggest issues in source criticism of the Gospels is the question of the relationship (in terms of literary dependence of one on another) of the Synoptic Gospels Matthew, Mark and Luke. It is often referred to as 'the synoptic problem': the three Gospels are in some places so alike that some sort of source-dependence seems certain, but which Gospel used which? The evidence is, broadly, as follows:
- there is very little that is in Mark that is not also in both Matthew and Luke;
- Matthew and Luke have some material in common that is not in Mark;
- Luke and Matthew each has material which is unique to their Gospel.

The solution for which there is now a broad scholarly consensus is the 'two-document hypothesis' associated with B H Streeter (1924). This theory is based on two ideas:
- Mark's Gospel was written first and was a source for Matthew and Luke;
- Matthew and Luke also had another source in common, now lost (known as 'Q' because *Quelle* is German for 'which'), and this was a collection of sayings of Jesus.

EXERCISE

☐ **Read Matthew 13:53–58 and Mark 6:1–6.** Look at the way the two verses below speak about the power of Jesus. The full passages give the context. This parallel is used by Tuckett (1987, p. 82).

Matthew 13:58	*Mark 6:5–6*
And he *did not* do many deeds of power there,	And he *could do no* deed of power there, except that he laid his hands on a few sick people and cured them. And he was *amazed at* their
because of their unbelief.	unbelief.

In this example, does it seem to you more likely that Matthew used Mark as a source or that Mark used Matthew?

Many scholars conclude that the parallel in the exercise above is an example of Matthew using Mark as a source. Matthew has slightly rephrased the passage to remove any implication, which is left open in Mark, that Jesus was powerless to act in the face of the people's lack of faith. Matthew's version suggests that Jesus made a choice not to exercise his power: the people's lack of faith is to blame, not Jesus' ability.

If Mark had used Matthew as a source here, he would have been consciously changing a sentence about Jesus' choice to one about his lack of power. It is harder to see why he might have done this than why Matthew might have changed it the other way. This is not by any means conclusive, but one small piece of evidence among much more.

Does it help us get back to the historical fact? Do we further conclude that Mark is right that Jesus lacked the power on this occasion, rather than chose not to use his power? This is where source criticism may not be the answer to the historical question. Mark's version, even if it did precede Matthew's version, is nevertheless a *version* of the story, which may or may not be recording what took place in Nazareth or (because the story does not say that Jesus himself commented on the affair) what took place in Jesus' thoughts and intentions.

Apart from the two-document hypothesis there are other theories of which Synoptic Gospel used which as a source, though none has such a large following as this. The original compilers of the canon of the New Testament suggest, by the order in which the Gospels are set out, that they give some sort of priority to Matthew. The oldest, pre-critical, theory is that the Gospels were written in the order they appear in the New Testament, and that each knew their predecessors. However, the question of sources did not really enter this view since the assumption seems to have been that all the Gospels were written by eye-witnesses, an assumption no longer held by many. There is a possible *historical* reason why Matthew might have been listed first: this is the Gospel in which Peter is given particular authority in the later church (see Matthew 16:13–19) and if church leaders, perhaps those in Rome, believed they had inherited this authority of Peter's, they might well have wanted Matthew's version to receive pride of place.

The other big source question in the Gospels is about the other Gospel: does John's Gospel use one or more of the earlier ones as a source or is it a completely independent tradition?

There is very little in John's Gospel that can be compared word by word and phrase by phrase with Synoptic parallels. The old view on this was that John knew the Synoptic Gospels and used them to convey a particular, spiritualised, theologised account of the historical events that the earlier Gospels record more factually. Nowadays, there is a greater consensus that all the Gospels have a theological and spiritual 'spin' to their accounts, not just John's. There is less agreement about how far John uses the earlier Gospels as sources, though. It may be wholly independent, though of course it draws on the same type of material, the 'units of tradition' that circulated first in oral form, as the other Gospels do.

Historically, the old argument used to be that when the Synoptics all give an account of an event and John's version differs, the Synoptics' three versions weigh against the single one, and John's must be unhistorical. If we accept a source hypothesis where Matthew and Luke are both using Mark, it turns out that only one version (Mark's) is weighed against John's, and we might decide that John's account has as much claim to be considered historical as the Synoptics'.

Is this investigation of sources valuable in determining historical events? It is clearly not a way to achieve a guarantee of historical reliability. It is often a useful stage of enquiry to undertake, but there is still a gap between the earliest source material and the events themselves. It is probably more illuminating *theologically* than historically: the process may unearth the Evangelists' ideas and theology when we see how one of them may have given a different 'spin' to a story than their source document did.

EXERCISE
📖 **Read again Matthew 13:58 and Mark 6:5–6.**

If we agree that Matthew's source was Mark, do we learn something from his rephrasing about Matthew's Christology? What do the changes suggest about Matthew's belief about and portrayal of Jesus?

Using form criticism for historical investigation

Form criticism was developed during the 1920s in part from the realisation that source criticism was not going to give the full and final answer on the historical events. The attention of some scholars turned instead to the earliest historical period that they felt they could unearth from the text, which was the oral stage, at least thirty or forty years, that must have occurred before the first Gospel was written. They looked at the separate small parts with which the whole text is made up, the small units of tradition like parables, miracle stories, dialogues and single sayings.

📖 **Read Mark 1:14–28.** Can you distinguish three separate units of tradition that the Evangelist has used here? There is a summary of Jesus' proclamation, a narrative of the call of four disciples, an account of Jesus teaching and healing. (Your translation probably divides the text up into these three paragraphs.)

A form critic deals with the shape of these individual units, and their separate history, and the development of the tradition (a study sometimes called tradition criticism) to explore how the units have been created, handed on, adapted before the Evangelist set them together in this sequence and context.

The basic idea is that there is a correlation between the way in which a formal unit (a story or saying) was told and a particular situation in the history of the first Christians to whom or by whom it was told. This situation is referred to as the *sitz im leben* (German for 'setting in the life').

📖 **Read Mark 12:13–17.** What is the most important verse in this story, the one which would have helped it to be remembered and passed on?

For the form critic Vincent Taylor, this is an example of a form he called a 'pronouncement story' (Tuckett, 1987, p. 97). These are characterised as stories which are very brief, have very little extra detail and lead up to a 'punchline', a single saying of Jesus which is the point of telling the whole story. So for him, the answer to the question above would be 12:17.

EXERCISE
In what situation (*sitz im leben*) would the first Christians have needed to shape, remember, retell this story (Mark 12:13–17)? It would make a good text for a sermon, certainly, and the form critic Dibelius, for example, suggests that the *sitz im leben* of such stories is in the preaching of the earliest churches.

Historically, it is a very speculative study. Did the first Christians distinguish so very carefully between one form of story and another, so that pronouncement stories were only used in sermons, while other forms, for example, individual sayings of Jesus like 1:15, were used on some different occasions for some different purpose? That is what the form critics build their theories on. It has to involve some historical guesswork about the particular contexts and activities of the first Christians.

The idea of separate units often taking particular *forms* is a useful investigation though, and useful historically as well as theologically.

To see this in action, we will move up to the next layer and the next tool.

Redaction criticism and historical investigation

☐ **Look again at Mark 1:14–15.** If 1:15 is a unit of tradition of a recognisable form (a single saying of Jesus used in whatever situation in the earliest churches), then 1:14 which precedes it is not necessarily part of the tradition as it came to Mark. Verse 14 is Mark's own writing, giving us a narrative setting for this summary proclamation of Jesus.

Historically, this is negative evidence: it means that we cannot rely on Mark to have passed on to us the earliest tradition of exactly when and where Jesus said this. However, *theologically* we may perceive important things about Mark's message. It means that Mark has consciously chosen to put this saying at the head of his Gospel and at the beginning of the ministry of Jesus. It is clearly Mark's intention to signal this as being the heart of Jesus' message and the key too to the message of this Gospel. He has chosen further to make a deliberate time reference to the death of John the Baptist: he is telling the reader that Jesus' ministry begins where John's left off, not just in terms of time-scale but in terms of its significance.

It is because of insights like this that many scholars conclude that the Gospels are intentionally theological writings rather than primarily historical ones.

The inability of form criticism to prove conclusively what part of the text could be attributed to the oral stage of development and transmission, and what should be attributed to the work of the Evangelist, led to a greater interest in the role of the individual Evangelists in shaping and arranging the material they received. In many ways the study moves us away from historical enquiry of sources, traditions and historical setting to an attention to the theological intention of the author.

Redaction (which means 'editing') criticism has a focus on the Evangelist's particular contribution to the way the units of tradition are selected, arranged, linked and summarised. There is an interest in the meaning of the Gospel as that intended by the Evangelist for his first readers or hearers, in their historical time and place. There are historical problems here, of course: we do not know who the Evangelists were, and we do not know when they wrote and the communities for whom they wrote! Any such information (on the whole) can only be inferred from the text of a Gospel itself.

In this historical 'layer' of the text, the communities of the Evangelists, there has also recently been an attention to *social history*. What some scholars seek is an accurate understanding of social, economic, political conditions prevailing in the first century in Palestine and the urban centres around the Mediterranean. This gives them a basis on which to make historical judgements about the situations described in the Gospels and the contexts in which and for which the Gospels may have been written.

Historical-critical study

The historical caution and scepticism of many of these 'historical-critical' methods means that they are viewed by some Christians as inappropriate because they appear not to honour the text as inspired scripture. There are issues here of truth and authority which go beyond the scope of the present study (but see chapter 8). However, there are also Christians who would argue that an appreciation of the historical issues, and of the gulf of history that separates the biblical texts from a reader today, is crucial to using the Bible.

📖 **Read these two passages from Isaacs (1991):**

> What for many is the principal weakness of historical exegesis *(interpretation)*, i.e. that it emphasises the distance between ourselves and the Bible, is, in my opinion, one of the major contributions to the preacher, since, for all her/his desire to reinterpret the text and make it meaningful for today, s/he must never forget that the text has an integrity of its own, which should not be manipulated, even in the interests of a good cause. By directing our attention to the original context of the text, the historical exegete *(interpreter)* reminds us that the Bible is not made in our image; it is foreign, and therefore needs to be listened to, not dictated to; to be translated, not tamed. Preachers who ignore the distinction between the world of the Bible and that of today end up either modernising the past or archaising the present.

> Potentially one of the most liberating insights of modern biblical studies for the preacher is an appreciation of the occasional nature *(texts written in and for specific circumstances)* of much of the Bible.

This is no ready-made book, but rather a collection of religious insights, originally delivered to a variety of specific situations. Since these situations differed in time, place and circumstance, inevitably the message changed accordingly ... The preacher should take heart from this, and neither be embarrassed by the diversity of the biblical witness, nor seek to hide it from the congregation ... The Christian believer needs the preacher to relate (this fact) to the on-going task of understanding the community's past inheritance in the light of the present, changing experience of faith.

EXERCISE

Do you agree that there may be problems if readers and interpreters of the Bible 'modernise the past': read ancient texts as if they were about the modern world?

How far is it important to see Jesus as a man of his own historical time and place?

Further reading

Theissen, G (1987), *The Shadow of the Galilean*, London, SCM.
Theissen, G and Merz, A (1998), *The Historical Jesus: a comprehensive guide*, London, SCM, pp. 1–11.

Source, form and redaction criticism
Tuckett, C (1987), *Reading the New Testament*, London, SPCK, chapters 6 to 8.
Sanders, E P and Davies, M (1989), *Studying the Synoptic Gospels*, London, SCM.

Historical-critical findings
Hooker, M D (1991), *The Gospel according to St Mark*, London, A and C Black.
Brown, R E, Fitzmyer, J A and Murphy, R E (eds) (1990), *The New Jerome Biblical Commentary*, London, Chapman.

Synoptic Gospels set out in parallel columns
Throckmorton, B H (ed.) (1979), *Gospel Parallels*, London, Nelson.

7. USING LITERARY SKILLS

Introduction

Literary approaches to biblical text are sometimes contrasted with historical-critical ones (chapter 6). This chapter looks at literary forms in the Bible in the context of understanding genre; and it illustrates some insights of literary approaches as one strategy of reading.

Reflecting on experience

What makes a good story? Consider one (a joke, a story line from a TV 'soap', a fairytale, an Agatha Christie, whatever)

Why have you remembered this particular one? How far was your appreciation of it influenced by *the way* it was told or written, and what it was *about*?

Narrative texts

In the previous chapter, the text and approaches to interpreting it were described as being an archaeological dig. The top layer and its 'tools' is the one this chapter investigates. Literary approaches are often contrasted with historical ones. They can be 'synchronic' (looking at the text without reference to historical events or to any history of its interpretation) rather than 'diachronic' (looking at the text as referring to historical events and having a history of tradition). However, the literary approach need not exclude the historical and theological interests we may have in the texts, and some of these are integrated in the examples investigated.

Because the focus of chapter 6 was the Gospels, the 'tools' described briefly there referred to investigating *narrative* texts, texts that tell a story. Not all the material in the Bible is narrative: for example, Paul is not often telling a story, he is usually making an argument. The literary tools for different genres, different types of writing, vary. When we employ literary skills on Paul's letters we are likely to be analysing his rhetoric, how he puts a point across, how he persuades.

It is important to be able to distinguish genre, and everybody does it, often without conscious analysis. Most of us have no trouble distinguishing that the nature of the material is different when we tune in to an episode of Channel 4 news from when we watch an episode of *Coronation Street*. They may both deal with long-running or week-long stories, and indeed trivia, mayhem and murder, but we respond in some ways differently because the programmes belong to different genres. When they get mixed up and the wrongful imprisonment of a fictional 'soap' character is reported on the news, we may be bemused.

There is an historical side to the question of literary genre. We may know about the genre of a television news programme and a serial drama: these are genres of our culture. The biblical texts sometimes reflect genres of writing which are not practised in our contemporary culture in the same way as in, say, the Roman empire in the first century CE.

This chapter is structured with a number of examples of types of biblical text where an understanding of the genre helps the reader interpret the text. When the genre is appreciated, the normal literary skills of the reader can then be used to read with understanding.

Narratives and collections of narratives

Some genres can cross boundaries of time and culture. A good story may be 'flavoured' with its particular history and culture but it can remain a good story for people of other lands and other centuries. Many genres use narrative, story, as the whole or part of their method of communicating, and these are often very accessible to a reader's usual literary skills.

These skills may be put in the form of the questions that, consciously or subconsciously, we ask as we read, some of which are as basic as who, what, when, where and how?

- What is the setting of the action? *(When? and Where?)*
- How are the people/actors portrayed? Are there protagonists and antagonists? *(Who? Characterisation)*
- What is happening and what are we being led to expect? *(What? Plot)*

- What means does the narrative use to get its message across? *(How? Style)*
- To whom does the narrative seem to be directed? *(Implied reader)*
- Does the teller of the story seem to have a viewpoint? *(Implied narrator)*

Some books of the Bible are composite, a collection of a number of stories woven together into a greater whole, rather than single, authored, texts. For example, Genesis 1 to 11, before the sequential sagas of Abraham, Jacob and Joseph begin, is made up of several, separable narratives. In sections like these, or even across the whole Book of Genesis, we might ask further questions such as:

- Is there a sequence of different sections? Is it a coherent whole with a beginning, middle and end? How are the parts linked together?
- Who are the chief characters in different sections?
- Are there main themes? (Are there key verses expressing these themes?)
- Are there particular types of literature here (for example, poetry, genealogy, saga, myth)?
- Why would people have collected/told/written these stories?

EXERCISE

'The medium is the message.' Pure narrative conveys its message not by authorial comment to the reader about what the story means but in the way, the sequence, the style, in which the story is told.

📖 Read Luke 1:5–38.

Here are two episodes, juxtaposed. In one, a priest at an altar in the Temple in Jerusalem is visited by a messenger of God and does not believe the message. In the second, an unmarried girl in an undistinguished town, a long way from the national centre of power and religion, is visited by the same angel and says, 'Let it be so.' What might be Luke's message to the reader in this juxtaposition?

Parable and allegory

The word 'parable' is used in the Bible to cover a number of types of story and sayings: proverbs, riddles, allegories, metaphors, example stories. All of these are uses of language that require the reader or listener to recognise a symbolic or metaphorical level to the words. Like all the metaphorical language we studied in chapter 5, parables depend on a 'perception of affinities': the reader must recognise that something in the story is like something else that is not being said explicitly.

Jesus seems characteristically to have used parables in his teaching. Good stories, of course, are memorable, and that may be reason enough. It is possible that the 'hidden' meaning in them may have helped him avoid the attention of the authorities for a while: if you are talking about the reign of God turning human government upside down, and a Roman soldier or a collaborator is listening, it may be wise to tell stories with symbolic language (Stein, 1993, p. 568). Probably, though, the most important thing about the method is the way stories like these can disarm listeners who may be resisting the message: we are drawn into the story and, before we discover our defences have been lowered, the message has penetrated. Story-telling is a developed oral or literary skill.

Though the word 'parable' is used to cover many types of story and saying, it is also a precise genre, and some of Jesus' stories fit the form. The basic idea is that whereas an allegory is a string of metaphors, a parable makes a single metaphor.

EXERCISE
📖 **Read Mark 4:30–32.**

What is the single, key similarity here between the reign of God and what happens to the mustard seed?

Parables are often effective if, on the face of it, the two things being compared are radically *dis*similar. The metaphorical 'jump' is an experience with an element of shock or laughter or a 'flash' of perception.

When the stories are longer there is a tendency, which seems an inevitable tendency of the literary mind or just the human mind, to find a *sequence* of metaphors, and to make an allegory. An allegory is a story where each character, item or event may represent someone or something else. If we tried to make an allegory, we would look for a comparison of each item in the story. Here is the example from Mark 4:31–32.

items in the story	*a 'string' of metaphors*
sowing the seed	= preaching the Gospel
large branches	= different churches founded by the apostles
birds of the air	= converts to Christianity
make nests	= find refuge and salvation

You may remember from chapter 2 that this was a favourite interpretative method of the medieval church. Does this work here? Is it what Jesus or Mark meant? With similarities and metaphors it is not always clear when the reader is to *stop* making links.

Sometimes a knowledge of the genre can guide the reader. There are some parables that cannot be intended as allegories because the 'string of metaphors' produces a comparison that goes against the apparent message of the teacher.

EXERCISE
📖 **Read Luke 18:2–5.**

Try allegorising this parable. Is there a problem with the character who, in an allegory, seems to represent God?

Treat it as a parable and look for a single point of comparison between praying and the widow's story.

There is a parable in the Gospels that either Jesus himself or those who retold his stories allegorised as well as telling the parable as a parable.

📖 **Read Mark 4:1–9 and then 4:13–20.**

Strictly speaking it does not work as an allegory. When you draw the lists of comparisons you find that in verse 14 the seed means the 'word' of the preacher. In the next verses the seed means instead the 'people who hear the word' of the preacher. This may suggest that when first told, the story belonged to the genre of parable rather than allegory. Its *parabolic* meaning is a bit like that of the mustard seed parable: the reign of God will be like a hundredfold harvest.

You have seen three examples of parables that work in a particular way if they are understood as being of a particular genre. You probably

did not need to know about the characteristic of the genre to understand the message; your literary skills dealt with the language, the
metaphor and the context of the story. However, are there insights to be
gained in distinguishing parables from the tendency to allegorise them?
The parable of the sower, allegorised, may not be an exact allegory, and
may lose some of the force of the parable as a parable, but it also carries
a message about the Gospel. The example of the parable of the unjust
judge, however, or rather the parable of the persistent petitioner, suggests some genre distinction is helpful. Perhaps the best advice is, seek
the main point first before going on to look for an additional 'string' of
correspondences.

Myth

In our culture if you ask for an explanation of, say, what distinguishes
human beings from other animals, or ask why different nations speak
different languages, you are more likely to be given some abstract
philosophy, or empirical biology or linguistic analysis, than you are to
be told a story. In other cultures, and the ancient Hebrew culture among
them, truth, meaning and understanding are often conveyed in the form
of a dynamic narrative, a story with characters and events and dialogue.
Among the narratives in Genesis that belong to this genre are two myths
of creation, 1:1 to 2:3 and 2:4–25; myths of humanity's disobedience,
3:1 to 4:26; a myth of judgement and salvation, 6:1 to 9:28; a myth about
the origin of national languages, 11:1–9.

Myths are stories which, like parable and allegory, are symbolic. They
are often about human experience in general. Their aim is often to
express a universal truth rather than a particular history. In contemporary English, the word 'myth' is often used to mean 'falsehood'. We need
to dismiss that meaning from our thinking when we are interpreting
biblical or other ancient myths because the point is not that they are 'fictitious' in the sense of untrue, but fictitious in the sense of creative stories of insight, explanation and truth. The question to be asked is not,
'Is this true or a myth?' but rather, 'Is this a true myth?', a story which
speaks truth about the created world, the human condition, the meaning of life.

Myths are more complex as symbolic stories than parables. Insights
embodied in a myth may be applied to every point of a person's life and
be a framework within which the whole of life may be understood
(Fawcett, 1970, p. 101). The myths of Genesis 1, 2 and 3, for example,

are meant to be overarching stories by which the events of one's own life story can, perhaps, be understood.

Where allegories may be understood by deciphering what each element of the story represents, there is not the same requirement to 'crack the code' of a myth. If we find a myth hard to understand it is likely to be because we do not share some cultural or linguistic association in the lives and minds of the myth-makers.

So, how do we read a myth? We use our usual literary skills of reading a story and may empathise with the characters and recognise the nature of the relationships and events described. We recognise also, however, that these events are in a world not our own. Myths are usually set in some time or place outside of the reader's own world: a place where, for instance, it is not regarded as odd for a serpent to speak or for God to 'walk in the garden'. The help we need, additional to our story-reading skills, may be the sort of information that footnotes and commentaries give us about cultural, linguistic, geographical matters that would have been open to the first hearers of the story. For example, Genesis 2:7 (*New Revised Standard Version*) reads:

God formed man from the dust of the ground.

A footnote gives us some of the Hebrew words:

God formed an *adam* from the *adamah*.

A commentary tells us further that the root of the words suggests 'reddy-brown' colour. This reveals a linguistic and a visual pun that we might have missed. The creation of humanity from the earth in the story reflects a connection apparent in the lives and language of the myth-maker: the correspondence of a human skin-tone with the colour of the soil, and the correspondence of a name for humankind with the word for the ground. We would have to translate, 'God made an earthy-one from the earth …' to get close to part of it in English.

EXERCISE
📖 **Read Genesis 3:1–13.**

Consider this narrative not as a picture of what may or may not have happened in history, in a garden, a long time ago, but as a representation of human beings of any time, of now. Make ▶▶

a list of features of the story that describe human reality, human responsibility and decision-making: what we are all like, and our characteristic responses to situations. Two examples are provided below.

• Being 'found out' is often accompanied by the feeling of exposure, of being 'naked'.

• 'Passing the buck': the man and the woman find someone else, the woman, God or the serpent, to blame.

Satire

The rather solemn way in which the Bible is often treated in Christian tradition may mislead us into reading some of the texts as solemn when, if we used our literary skills, they might properly move us to laughter. The Book of Jonah is no less a part of sacred scripture for being a fictional story, sharply satirical about the hypocrisy of its fearful and angry 'prophet' (Holbert, 1996).

An awareness of genre can alert us to the fact that it is very unusual for a book of a prophet to be so empty of the content of the prophet's message. This, instead, is a book *about* the prophet. There are many signs for the reader to grasp how the story is meant to be received. For some we may need some help with the Hebrew, or with local geography or other matters familiar to the first audience or readers. 'Jonah son of Amittai' (1:1) means 'Dove, the son of faithfulness' which sets up an expectation of a first-class prophet, and that expectation is defeated in the first thing Jonah does. To recognise the stark juxtaposition of call and response we might also need to know the local geography: where Nineveh, Joppa and Tarshish are in relation to Palestine. ('Get up and go to the East,' said God. So Jonah shot off down to the West.)

Some of the literary clues can get lost where the tradition of biblical translation does not convey the humour, or the style of expression. There is a series of grotesque or fantastic expressions and events, still characteristic of modern satire and even pantomime. God *hurls* a *great* wind at the sea, and there is a *great* storm, and the sailors *hurl* the cargo at the sea – while Jonah is fast asleep in the hold. The ship itself 'thinks' it is going to break up (1:4–5) (Holbert, 1997). Instead of dealing with the 'evil' in Nineveh (1:2), Jonah has brought this 'evil' (1:7) on another set of pagans. Moreover, these pagans turn out to be rather more pious than Jonah has been.

There are more satirical excesses. For example, Nineveh is described as being so huge it takes 'three days' to cross (3:3), though archaeology suggests a radius of three miles. There is a 'king of Nineveh' (3:6), though it was not a city-state with a king. The repentance of the city is so huge that the animals dress in sackcloth too and 'cry mightily to God'!

It might have puzzled the author of this book to see it read as a history of a pious prophet who learned an important lesson. It is rather more powerful as a book whose central character is shown, under the judgement and mercy of God, to have less true piety than a crew of sailors and the city of Nineveh (when Nineveh was a byword for wickedness).

EXERCISE
📖 **Read the Book of Jonah.**

Can you recognise some of the satirical features of the story? How far does the translation you use bring out any of the 'grotesque' or 'fantastic' elements of the story? What is the message?

Poetry

There are many examples of Hebrew poetry and song in the Old Testament. The Book of Psalms, of course, is wholly in this genre.

The interpretation of the Psalms in the church illustrates some of the difference between analysis that is more literary or more historical. Some of the psalms have a particular historical context or origin. How much does this affect the way we read it? Some, particularly those attributed to King David, may reflect a psalmist's responses to a specific incident. For example, Psalm 34 is headed, 'Of David, when he feigned madness before Abimelech, so that he drove him out, and he went away'. The incident referred to is in 1 Samuel 21:10–15 (though the Philistine king is called Achish there and not Abimelech). The biographical reference does not seem a close match for the sentiments of the psalm and is likely to be a later ascription. The experience prompting a psalmist to compose this psalm may be discoverable, in general terms, from the text itself, for example, in verses 4–6: 'I sought the Lord, and he answered me, and delivered me from all my fears' (Psalm 34:4). This psalm has surely found readers whose experiences and beliefs match those recorded here, and who read the psalm without reference to a more specific historical incident. Because some of the genres of poetry and song are recited or sung, it is often the case that the performance of the words becomes, or seems to become, a statement newly made by the reader or singer, expressing their own heart and mind, rather than recording an historical event.

EXERCISE
📖 **Read Psalm 34** (perhaps aloud).

How far do you find yourself participating in the sentiments, relief and thanksgiving of the psalmist in saying the same words with him/her? How far do these responses have their source in one or more of the following:
• your own particular experiences;
• a general human condition you share with the psalmist;
• an understanding of the psalmist's historical situation?

Another historical context of some psalms, which may inform or be in tension with our more purely literary responses, is the context of worship in the Jerusalem Temple. Some of the psalms seem to have been composed for use in liturgical processions or with such occasions in mind. For example, Psalm 24 with its question-and-answer refrain, ' Lift up your heads, O gates! and be lifted up, O ancient doors! that the King of glory may come in' (Psalm 24:7), may reflect a processional response at the gates of the Temple when the Ark of the Covenant was carried up to the sanctuary. Taken out of this context, the allusion to 'gates' becomes more thoroughly symbolic. In Christian use, there is probably a conscious or unconscious substitution of 'the gates of heaven' as a metaphor.

Poetry is not a single genre but takes many forms and there are specific features of verse in different traditions. One that can affect our interpretation is 'parallelism' or 'doublets'. Hebrew verse is often characterised by 'doublets', phrases that effectively repeat the previous phrase but with variations of words. Sometimes the variations are slight, and sometimes the idea develops slightly in the doublet.

EXERCISE
📖 **Read Psalm 8.**

How many parallel phrases can you find where a similar idea is repeated in different words?

There are doublets like these in Zechariah 9:9:

> Rejoice greatly, O daughter Zion! Shout aloud, O daughter Jerusalem!
> Lo, your king comes to you; triumphant and victorious is he,
> humble and riding on a donkey, on a colt, the foal of a donkey.

If we did not appreciate the function of doublets, we might on the face of it assume that Zion and Jerusalem were two different cities rather than two names for the same one. The Evangelist Matthew can take a rather literal (rather than literary) view about the Hebrew scriptures and he does something very like this. When he tells the story of Jesus riding triumphantly but humbly into Jerusalem, he cites this verse from Zechariah. In his source for this story, Mark's Gospel, Jesus tells his followers to collect a donkey for him to ride. Matthew, influenced by what he sees as an exact fulfilment of the words in Zechariah, has Jesus ask for a donkey and a colt, so 'they brought the donkey and the colt ... and he sat on them' (Matthew 21:7). It seems to be Matthew's way of showing that Jesus exactly fulfilled this poetic prophecy, but it is a reading of text that does not apply a recognition of doublets, characteristic of the genre.

There is poetic or psalmic writing in the New Testament, too. There seem to be fragments of some early Christian hymns in some of our texts. Philippians 2:6–11 seems to have characteristics of a poem or a hymn. Part of it (2:10–11 'At the name of Jesus') has been used as a modern hymn too. Colossians 1:15–20 may incorporate two stanzas of a hymn, the first to Jesus as the 'firstborn of creation' and the second to him as 'firstborn of the resurrection', of the new creation.

Again, specific characteristics of a poetic genre may influence our text. You have probably noticed in most English translations how rhythmical the opening of John's Gospel is. Parts of it may be a hymn, and some verses have a feature called 'climactic parallelism' or 'staircase parallelism' (Brown, 1971, p. 19). This is where a word in one line (usually near the end) is repeated in the next line (usually near the beginning).

You can find this in the Old Testament (Psalm 96:13) and elsewhere in John (6:37, 8:32) but it is in this 'prologue' to the Gospel that it is most sustained and effective. If we set out John 1:3–5 as follows, you can see the 'staircase' effect of moving up from one word or phrase to another:

> All things came into being *through the Word*
> and *apart from the Word* not a thing *came to be*.
> What *came to be* in the Word was *life*,
> and this *life* was the people's *light*.
> The *light* shines on in the *darkness*
> for the *darkness* did not overcome it.

The poetic form is a clue to the rhythmic and climactic power of the opening of the Gospel.

Paul's letters

Paul's letters follow the conventions of the time for formal letters, and have a characteristic pattern (Ziesler, 1990): first there is the greeting, then a thanksgiving, then an opening to the body of the letter followed by the body of the letter, and it closes with personal greetings and a blessing. Moreover, the body of the letter is often in two sections: the first is theoretical teaching and the second practical teaching, often ethical exhortation. For example, Romans 12 opens the 'second part' with a 'Therefore ...' or 'So ...' which indicates the transition from theoretical teaching to application and ethics.

EXERCISE

📖 **Read Philemon** (unless you are feeling ambitious and want to try a longer Pauline letter).

Identify the verses which seem to make up the following:
- salutation (writer, recipient, greeting);
- thanksgiving;
- opening of body of letter;
- theoretical part;
- practical/ethical part;
- closing (greetings, benediction).

> **EXERCISE**
> 📖 **Read Galatians 1:1–9.** Paul, characteristically, uses the greeting to describe himself in a way that indicates what his position is in the matter in hand. Here he separates himself already from the views of those like Cephas (Peter) whom he thinks are wrong (2:11).
>
> What is missing from Paul's usual pattern? This absence is a clue to how angry Paul is in this letter and how seriously he regards the congregation's teaching and practice concerning Jews and Gentiles in the church.
>
> Note how the first couple of verses after the thanksgiving (though here straight after the greeting because of the absence of the thanksgiving) work almost as the title or heading to what the letter is about. This is very useful, especially in a long letter like Romans or one dealing with many issues like 1 Corinthians. Try identifying these key verses in a couple of other Pauline letters, immediately after the thanksgiving.

Paul is writing letters with a view to persuading his churches to share his point of view, and he uses a number of rhetorical devices. He uses a style known as 'dialectic', particularly in Romans and 1 Corinthians. This is where he asks a question as if of a second person, and then answers it himself (see, for example, Romans 6:1–2). It is a way of getting the reader/listener involved in the argument, as if they were participating in it. In this way Paul hopes to 'bring the reader across' to share his opinion.

With rhetoric, it is a literary skill to ask not only 'What is the writer saying?' but 'What is the writer doing?' Paul writes that he will not 'command' Philemon to do as he asks (Philemon 8–9) because he wants Philemon to act freely and not as a response to his authority. This appears to leave Philemon free to choose, but does it? The reader has to remember that the sending of the letter is itself an act of authority. A parody of the position would be, 'You must choose freely for yourself but this is my view and I know you will agree with it.' Also, the letter greets the whole church so would have been read out publicly. What pressure would that put Philemon under? Is Paul manipulative? His personality comes across as passionate rather than calculating. He certainly was, and is, very persuasive: a master of rhetoric.

Further reading

Literary criticism

Davies, M (1990), Literary Criticism, in R J Coggins and J L Houlden (eds), *A Dictionary of Biblical Interpretation*, London, SCM.

Dennis, T (1991), *Lo and Behold! – the power of Old Testament storytelling*, London, Blackwell.

Longman, T (1987), *Literary Approaches to Biblical Interpretation*, Oxford, Apollos.

Tuckett, C (1987), *Reading the New Testament: methods of interpretation*, London, SPCK, pp. 174–183.

Myth, parable and allegory

Otzen, B and Gottlieb, H (1980), *Myths in the Old Testament*, London, SCM.

and articles from:

Metzger, B M and Coogan, B M (eds) (1993), *The Oxford Companion to the Bible*, Oxford, Oxford University Press.

Brown, R E, Fitzmyer, J A and Murphy, R E (eds) (1990), *The New Jerome Biblical Commentary*, London, Chapman.

Green, J B, McKnight, S and Marshall, I H (eds) (1992), *Dictionary of Jesus and the Gospels*, Leicester, IVP.

8. READERS AND BELIEVERS

Introduction

The focus of this chapter is the close relation of belief and religious tradition to understanding and applying biblical text. It considers the role biblical interpretation has had in the faith of the church and, conversely, the role that Christian faith has in the ways people interpret the Bible. Jewish believers also read and interpret the books, and these traditions are considered both in their own right and in relation to Christian interpretation. Bible stories are sometimes used to nurture the faith of children. This chapter looks at some of the interpretation that takes place in this practice.

We have already met a number of issues of belief in the discussion of the material and methods in previous chapters. There cannot be many questions in biblical interpretation that are *not* relevant to a discussion of Christian believers and their use of the Bible, but for some texts, some contexts and some methods of interpretation, such a discussion may be at the top of our agenda.

Reflecting on experience

Consider some other, very different, writings that some people may 'believe in' such as astrological horoscopes (the sort published in daily or weekly papers and magazines). Recall any conversations you may have had with people who believe or partly believe them, and conversations with people who think they are nonsense or worse.

What range of attitudes to these horoscopes could you describe? What sort of things do people on either side of the argument give as evidence for their belief or non-belief? What are the difficulties in discussing them when people differ about how true or false they are, and how harmless or harmful?

The Bible, the church and the world

In chapter 3 we saw how New Testament authors used scripture in their own writing, constructing and interpreting from Old Testament texts which were often read as messianic prophecy, proof-texts of Christian belief. When the New Testament writings themselves became a new, second, canon of scripture for the church, these texts too were drawn on for mission, apologetics (defending the faith in disputes), the creeds (agreed statements of belief) and for liturgy, the worship of the church.

The church is sometimes seen as drawing on three or four sources of authority: scripture, tradition and reason (and some would add experience). These are more interrelated than they may at first appear. Church tradition has (in various degrees) used scripture in formulating its teachings and practice; conversely, the New Testament scriptures were written *within* first-century Christian tradition: they are part of the earliest 'handing on' of teaching which is what 'tradition' means. Reason and experience do not stand apart from scripture either: reasoning and experience on the part of those who wrote the texts has shaped the texts we read and interpret, using in turn our reason and our experience.

Christian interpretation and application of the Bible, then, engages with and responds to the Bible (scripture), the church (tradition) and the world (taking human reason and experience of the created world as being included in the one word, 'world'). These are the 'shorthand' terms that will be used in some of the discussion that follows.

The Bible and the world

📖 **Read Luke 10:25–37.** The lawyer asked Jesus for an interpretation of scripture, and then for a definition of the category 'neighbour', whom the law requires him to love. Jesus in reply offers not a definition of a neighbour but a description of a neighbourly act, between people who were, definitively, held not to be 'neighbours'. Moreover, the final statement in the episode is not, 'Which was a neighbour?' but, 'Go and do the same.'

This interpretation by Jesus of scriptural teaching on two commandments from the Torah is one rooted firmly in the world as well as in the Bible. His parables and other teachings draw on the everyday experiences of his audience: 'Suppose one of you has a friend ...' (Luke 11:5); 'Which one of you, having a hundred sheep ...?' (Luke 15:3). Often, as in all these examples, the response to his teaching seems to demand not so much a pious spiritual belief but some action, doing something in the world. In a way, all the biblical texts are like this: they arise from experience and action and they lead to experience and action.

There are forms of biblical interpretation that are less directly engaged with the world the reader lives in and which might lead less directly to action.

EXERCISE
📖 **Look again at Luke 10:25–37.**

Remember the distinction made in chapter 7 between reading a text as parable (a single metaphor) or as an allegory (a string of metaphors).

The medieval church favoured the allegorical method (part of the fourfold method they used. Here is the string of resemblances that they discovered or created in the story of the Good Samaritan (Stein, 1993, p. 568).

Substitute these ideas into the story and consider the meaning of the story that results. What is gained? What is lost?
• man = Adam/humanity
• Jericho = our mortality
• Jerusalem = heaven
• robbers = the devil and his angels
• the priest = the law
• the Levite = the prophets
• the Samaritan = Christ
• beast/donkey = the body of Christ
• an inn = the church
• two denarii = love commands (10:27)
• the innkeeper = the apostle Paul
• return of the Samaritan = resurrection or second coming

This is unlikely to be the meaning that *Luke* thought the story had, because his setting is the question that the lawyer asks, and the allegory loses sight of what it means to act as a neighbour.

In this example the Bible and the church are both used as sources for the meaning. It is the church's understanding of the salvation of Adam or humanity, by Christ and in the church, that is read in(to) this story. The interpretation is related to the world of the reader only in a theoretical way. It is as if Jesus were to say after the story not, 'Go and do the same' but, 'That is how to think about the doctrine of salvation.' This evaluation is not meant to denigrate this imaginative use of the story to teach Christian doctrine: the medieval allegory is an insightful and powerful interpretation. Moreover, remember that this was only one of the four methods of interpretation used in the medieval church, and one of the other methods would find the practical implications of the text. If our interpretation of texts were always to take place without reference to the world we live in and what we do in it, for example, loving our neighbours and our enemies, it would surely not be the full version of what is meant by 'Christian interpretation'. We might go further and say that unless the reader then *acts* as such a neighbour in the world, then the Bible has not been interpreted by a Christian, only read by a reader.

The same might be said of interpretation where only the Bible is considered and not its understanding in the church nor its application in the world. This might be a criticism made of either *purely historical-critical* investigation or *purely literary* analysis of texts. These can remain wholly in the realm of history or literature, and not all readers choose to take this interpretation beyond the historical horizon or literary style of the text. For the reader who is also a believer, the historical and literary skills are the means but not the end. Interpretation of the Bible that is, say, knowledgeable about ancient Samaritan beliefs, linguistic puns in myths, or Hebrew verse forms, may be invaluable as part of what we need. It does not, however, give all that the reader/believer needs if they seek an interpretation of the Bible that speaks in the church and to the world.

The Bible and the church

Nevertheless, a clarity about what the Bible says, *apart* from what the church says, may also be thought to be the proper task of anyone studying the Bible. There can be a 'dialogue' of two distinct voices between the expressions of Christian doctrine and what the words of the Christian scriptures say. There are times when the interpreters of the Bible have found meanings other than those given to it in Christian tradition. The past, and sometimes present, church teachings on the subordination of women, to men in general and to their husbands in particular, often use texts (for example from Genesis 3 and 1 Corinthians 14) to give authority to this view. The texts themselves may well not justify this view, and moreover there are other texts and approaches to reading which challenge it further. (There is more on gender and biblical interpretation in chapter 9.) Biblical interpretation sometimes claims the freedom to find in the Bible meanings other than those that church tradition has seen in it.

This is an old debate (outlined in part in chapter 2) and a new one too. In the period of the Reformation, the Protestant challenge of *'sola scriptura'* (truth revealed by 'scripture alone') made a claim for biblical authority over against the doctrine of the church. In time, of course, the Protestant Reformed traditions too (new churches) guided or determined the interpretation of the Bible in those communities. The post-Enlightenment critical interpretation again challenged church teachings, using historical methods on the texts. The debate is still lively today because some of the methods, particularly literary methods of interpretation, are undertaken without reference to history or theology, or Christian and Jewish readings of the text. For some believers, biblical interpretation should concern itself primarily with the theological issues raised by the texts within the context of today's church and today's world. For others, both inside and outside Christian or Jewish communities of faith, biblical interpreters have no responsibility to read the text in the light of, say, Lutheran orthodoxy, or as supporting a particular teaching of Vatican II Catholicism.

The relationship between the Bible and the church can be conceptualised in three different ways:
- The Bible is located wholly *within* the church and is properly interpreted by it alone.
- The Bible is one thing, the church is another. They are discussed separately from one another.
- The Bible and the church are neither identical nor autonomous. They are interrelated with each informing the other, but they are also in 'dialogue' as separate authorities. Church teaching is not derived from the Bible alone. Biblical interpretation may take place outside the church (and this may challenge *or* add to its teachings). It also takes place inside the church.

How you read can depend on what you believe

People have perspectives, including religious perspectives, and 'What you see depends on where you stand'. Different people can bring different religious assumptions and beliefs to the same text and come away each with their original beliefs confirmed.

For example, in nineteenth-century England when the trend in biblical studies was the 'quest of the historical Jesus' (discussed in chapter 6) a number of liberal Protestant authors wrote 'A Life of Jesus'. At the end of the century Albert Schweitzer reviewed these books and concluded that each of these portraits of Jesus displayed the personality which in the eyes of the different authors was the ethical or spiritual ideal most worth striving for (Theissen and Merz, 1998, p. 5). That is, they had all *projected* their preconceived ideal onto the character they claimed to be *discovering*. There is a memorable statement of this tendency (that all readers share) to project their own circumstances and beliefs into biblical texts. Harnack was one of the liberal Protestant authors who looked in the Gospel texts for the 'true' face of Jesus, and a critic wrote later: 'The Christ that Harnack sees, looking back through nineteen centuries of Catholic darkness, is only the reflection of a liberal Protestant face, seen at the bottom of a very deep well (Tyrell, 1910, p. 49).'

This example warns us that we are not objective readers. Indeed, there is no interpretation that is free from presuppositions of some sort, because none of us is merely 'a blank canvas' without experiences and beliefs that colour our thinking. We interpret the Bible in relation to, or in dialogue with, the church and the world.

For many Christians, a theological reading which is centred on the belief of the church is a 'touchstone' for biblical interpretation. An evangelical Christian heard a sermon from a well-known Protestant minister and politician of rigid views and said, 'It was thoroughly biblical and the doctrine was "sound", but it can't have been right because there was no love in the message.' For her, a theology of love is an interpretative principle to use on the Bible. Indeed, in the interdependent relationship of church and Bible, the Bible itself provides justification for such a principle (for example, 1 Corinthians 13).

In many ways, as in this example, our beliefs influence our reading of the Bible, just as our reading of the Bible influences our belief. This is true also of the stage before we read it, the translations that we read. These cannot be wholly objective but are influenced by the belief and assumptions of the translators and editors (see chapter 1), who may then influence us.

EXERCISE

Compare these translations of Genesis in modern versions. Both are scholarly and use the best manuscripts and expertise in Hebrew. The *New International Version* is a translation which subscribes to an evangelical doctrine and a particular belief in the 'infallibility' of the Bible. The *New Revised Standard Version* is more broadly ecumenical.

Genesis 1:6 and 8
- *New International Version* And God said, 'Let there be an expanse between the waters to separate water from water'. ... God called the expanse 'sky'.
- *New Revised Standard Version* And God said, 'Let there be a dome in the midst of the waters, and let it separate the waters from the waters.' ... God called the dome Sky.

Genesis 1:20
- *New International Version* And God said, 'Let the water teem with living creatures ...'
- *New Revised Standard Version* And God said, 'Let the waters bring forth swarms of living creatures ...'

Genesis 2:7–8
- *New International Version* ... the man became a living being. Now the LORD God had planted a garden ...
- *New Revised Standard Version* ... the man became a living being. And the LORD God planted a garden ...

Highlight the differences. Can you relate any of these to matters of belief?

The creation stories in Genesis are a battlefield for a lot of the debate about science and religion, and the historical or cosmological reliability of the accounts of creation. Arguably, the *New International Version* is concerned to defend the agreement of these accounts with a modern understanding of the nature of the cosmos and also to reconcile any apparent internal inconsistencies in the accounts.

Genesis 1:6 and 8 seem to describe an ancient world-view where a dome (*New Revised Standard Version*) or firmament (KJV) is fixed like a vast garden 'cloche' above a flat earth. The *New International Version* reflects a consciousness of a modern world-view in the word used to translate this. The *New International Version* assumption is that this account of creation is not necessarily a mythological way of writing but is consistent with scientific cosmology.

Genesis 1:20 may reflect the ancient understanding that water is capable of generating life, not merely sustaining it. The *New International Version* translation is ambiguous ('teem' can mean both 'swarm with' as well as 'bear/bring forth') and so a reader of this translation may avoid this unscientific implication.

Genesis 2:7–8 are, many scholars think, part of a different account of creation. There seem to be two accounts of creation, Genesis 1:1 to 2:3 and 2:4–24. In the first, the creation of vegetation (1:12) precedes the creation of humanity (1:27), and in the second account, humanity is created (2:7) before the vegetation (2:9). The *New Revised Standard Version* allows each account to tell its story without reconciling this, while the *New International Version* uses a verb tense in 2:8 which indicates that the garden had already been planted.

EXERCISE

Do you have a view on the appropriate method of translation in texts like these? How far should a translation foster a reader in a particular tradition of belief and how far should it leave the text open to interpretations which do not accord with that tradition?

The key place of history in Christian interpretation

Christians vary in the importance they ascribe to historical truth in the Bible. For some, for example, the creation stories in Genesis are accurate accounts of how the world came into being while for others they are not intended as scientific or factual accounts but are mythological truths about the relationships of God and humanity and the created order. The spectrum of Christian beliefs about the Gospels is probably much narrower. There cannot be many who subscribe to Christian belief who do not think it important whether or not a first-century Jewish man called Jesus (or Yeshua) lived, taught, healed, was arrested and put to death, and that his followers proclaimed him raised to new life. We might agree that we would be very *edified* by reading about a fictional character in a novel by Mark who did these things, but most readers who are believers will hold that the character and the events refer to things outside the world of the text, and which belong both to the history of first-century Palestine, and to a spiritual 'reality'.

There is a range of views among Christian readers about whether the historical figure, Jesus, said everything he is recorded as saying, and exactly in the contexts that the Gospels narrate. There will be different views on how far the oral tradition or the Evangelists' interpretations have constructed or developed what is recorded. There is likely, nonetheless, to be a very large measure of agreement among this community of readers that historical-critical tools should be among those used, on the Gospels and on other biblical texts too.

Jewish belief and reading the Bible

Because this book is part of a series exploring issues of Christian faith, the concerns and traditions of Christian interpretation are the major matter. However, the distinctive approaches of Jewish tradition in the interpretation of the Tanakh may be illuminating as we consider readers and believers.

The classical tradition of interpretation in Judaism is called Midrash. The midrashim were commentaries produced in the rabbinic schools of Palestine between CE 70 and 500. These are argumentative, explanatory and, fascinatingly, often contradictory, because the opinions of different scholars are quoted even though their views differ. Scripture is not thought to have one single, fixed and original meaning: it can mean many things at once. Even if two contradictory conclusions are drawn from one text, both can be read as 'words of the living God' (Alexander, 1993, p. 307).

For the rabbis the canon of scripture is closed and prophecy has ceased. The scribe replaces the prophet as the role of authority. However, the rabbis in maintaining their authority did elevate their interpretations to much the same status as scripture. The rabbis were viewed as inspired and their interpretations became Oral Torah (Alexander, 1993). (Church doctrines have sometimes had a similar status in Christian traditions.)

The seventeenth to nineteenth centuries saw the same growth of interest in the analysis of language and the historical origins of the biblical writings that marked the controversies in Christian tradition.

In the twentieth century the Holocaust, referred to by many Jews as the 'Shoah' ('Destruction'), with its death-camps and systematic attempt at entire genocide, has become an experience by which scripture must be interpreted. The Shoah has a status like the remembered and 're-lived' experiences of the exodus and the exile.

EXERCISE

📖 **Read Exodus 16:1–3 and 17:1–4.** Moses criticises the Israelites for complaining in the wilderness: he calls them a 'stiff-necked people' (34:9) and says they are not complaining against him but against God (16:8). The narrator of Exodus implicitly sides with Moses and with God against their complaining.

Now read what Emil Fackenheim (1990) writes about these passages, with a post-Holocaust perspective:

> As this is read by Jews of this generation, they perceive just how radically their religious station has changed; they have no choice but to take sides with the mothers of the children, against the narrator, against Moses and, if necessary, against God himself.

This is a reading which takes seriously the world and the reality of human experience, as well as the Bible.

In chapter 3 you examined the Christian interpretation of Isaiah 53 in Matthew's Gospel. This is an example of the difference between Jewish and Christian readings. Christian readings of Old Testament texts are often messianic and Christological. That is, they read texts as prophecies of the Messiah who was promised, and they found the fulfilment of the prophecies in Jesus. Often Jewish readings of the same texts do not assume that the texts are messianic prophecy. The 'Suffering Servant' in Isaiah, for example, can be interpreted as representing Israel.

As well as a tradition of interpretation of the Tanakh, in recent years Jewish scholars have also commented on the Christian New Testament. This has coincided with a growing appreciation among Christian readers of the thoroughly Jewish character of Jesus, his teaching, his followers, the early church and the Jewish patterns of biblical interpretation in the New Testament. It has heightened the questions of the real or apparent anti-Jewish expressions in parts of the Gospels. Three accounts of

Jesus in Jewish research from the beginning of the twentieth century represent Jesus as an ethicist (Klausner, 1907), a prophet (Montefiore, 1909) and as a rebel (Eisler, 1927) (see Theissen and Merz, 1998, p. 9.) These are insightful contributions to New Testament Christology.

Bible stories for children

The first authors and editors of the books of the Bible almost certainly did not have an audience of children in mind. They are adult books, and the ancient cultures in many ways focused less on the development of children than we do today. The use of story to convey so much of the matter makes some parts of the Bible apparently accessible to young children as well as to adults. Is this really so?

Story makes a great workshop and playground for the imagination, and imagination is surely essential in the development of religious understanding. Story-telling also leads to 'open-ended' interpretation where there is not one, closed, interpretation but different readers may take different meanings from a text. Should children be guided to one meaning or be allowed to make what they will of a biblical story?

Stories can offer children the opportunity to think about, and empathise with, characters. However, there are probably few biblical characters whose stories are really suitable for the world and understanding of a young child. Most collections of Bible stories for children are very selective about which stories are chosen and also very selective about what meaning is to be conveyed.

EXERCISE
📖 **Read Genesis 9:18–25; 2 Samuel 11:2–5 and Luke 12:42–53.**

Would you leave these stories until teenage years or could you tell the stories in an appropriate way to younger children? Why would you offer or withhold them?

Are all the stories about Noah, David and even Jesus, ones you would choose to read to children? (There is no shortage of sex and violence in scripture.)

The question of 'stages' of faith development in children has been studied and there are insights in this enquiry for how a child may interpret a story. Does it matter if a story is presented as 'true' or, like some folk and fairy stories, not entirely or not at all true? Do we present the story of Jonah and the big fish as a story or as history? Is that story to be treated differently from the story of an angel speaking to Mary (Luke 1), or of Jesus' resurrection (Matthew 28)?

The same issues that inform or limit an adult reading of a story can be important in a child's understanding too. Some of the historical skills must be offered to a child: for example, the meaning of the story of Zacchaeus (Luke 19:1–10) probably requires some child-sized explanation of the role and status of tax-collectors and the attitudes of people to them in first-century Roman-occupied Palestine. The focus of the Bible on men rather than women may not be the perspective we wish our children to perpetuate; and until they have some of the adult skills to deal with this (see chapter 9) we might want to select and retell stories in a more inclusive way. The same may be true of the racial perspectives.

EXERCISE

Compare these passages from two different editions of *The Children's Bible in 365 Stories* published by Lion. Were these revisions appropriate? (See chapter 9 for further discussion of anti-semitism and the New Testament.)

Prior edition

- The Jewish teachers were strict about keeping the Ten Commandments, including the one that says, 'Do not murder.' But there were murderous thoughts against Jesus in their hearts.

Revised edition

- The religious teachers were strict about keeping the Ten Commandments, including the one that says, 'Do not murder.' But many of them had murderous thoughts against Jesus in their hearts.

The racial discrimination of Old Testament books in favour of Israel against the other inhabitants of Palestine (whose descendants share with Jews the land of Israel today) may be a prejudice we do not wish our children to practise. The anti-Jewish perspective in the Gospels also carries dangers and needs careful handling (and arguably this is no less true for adults than children – see chapter 9).

Whenever a story is retold, with new words and out of the context in which it is set in the version in the Bible, a new meaning may emerge. Some of the versions of Bible stories for children do not seem to have the same theological message as the versions of these stories in the Bible. The many retellings for children of 'David and Goliath' tend to emphasise the character of the boy David. He is, moreover, often portrayed in the pictures accompanying the story as being of an age with the children for whom the story is targeted, though in the text he is a 'stripling' (1 Samuel 17:56), a young man rather than a boy. The result is often that the retold story seems to be about David's heroism, about courage and skill in the face of danger. While this is an element in the biblical narrative of 1 Samuel 17, it is probably secondary. David is not here the hero-soldier: that role belongs to Saul (or even Goliath). The main point, and the underlying theology, seems rather that human greatness counts as nothing, but victory comes through the might or grace of God. This is the message in David's speech in 1 Samuel 17:45–47: God can use even an instrument as unlikely and as unheroic as David to bring victory over Israel's enemies.

The suitability of this story for children, however told (see, for example, 1 Samuel 17:52–54), is another matter. It is worth reflecting on how far two of the stories most frequently retold for children differ from the stuff of video 'nasties': the wholesale destruction of life in the Great Flood (Genesis 6–9) and this slaughter of Goliath and the Philistines (1 Samuel 17).

The authority of scripture

Here is the view of one Christian scholar on reading and believing (Barr, 1993a).

> Scripture, though understood to be the word of God, is in human language (Hebrew, Aramaic and Greek) and in the literary, rhetorical and poetic patterns of human expression, which can and must be interpreted by human understanding. God speaks through scripture, but its meanings function within the strictures of ordinary human language ... Approached in this way, the Bible is sometimes found to have

meanings other than those that traditional or superficial interpretations have suggested. Criticism is thus 'critical', not in the sense that it
'criticises' the Bible (it often reveres it as the basic and holy text), but
in the sense that it assumes freedom to derive from the Bible, seen in
itself, meanings other than those that traditional religion has seen in
it. Biblical criticism thus uncovers new questions about the Bible, even
as it offers fresh answers in place of old solutions.

EXERCISE
Do you agree with James Barr that it is appropriate for biblical criticism to challenge Christian tradition? What for you is the relationship of the church's teaching and the interpretation of the
Bible?

Further reading

Christian faith and the Bible
Noll, M A (1991), *Between Faith and Criticism: evangelicals, scholarship, and the
Bible*, Leicester, Apollos.
Watson, F (1990), Christian interpretation of the Old Testament, in R J Coggins
and J L Houlden (eds), *Dictionary of Biblical Interpretation*, London, SCM.
Metzger, B and Coogan, M D (eds) (1994), *Oxford Companion to the Bible*,
Oxford, Oxford University Press. See articles such as 'Inspiration and inerran-
cy' by W H Barnes, 'History of interpretation: modern biblical criticism' by J
Barr, 'Authority of the Bible' by R Hammer.

Jewish biblical interpretation
Magonet, J (1991), *A Rabbi's Bible*, London, SCM.
Magonet, J (1995), How do Jews interpret the Bible today?, *Journal for the Study of
the Old Testament*, 66, pp. 3–27.
Loewe, R (1990), Jewish exegesis, in R J Coggins and J L Houlden (eds), *Dictionary
of Biblical Interpretation*, London, SCM.

Christian faith, children and the Bible
Astley, J and Francis, L J (eds) (1992), *Christian Perspectives on Faith Development:
a reader*, Leominster, Gracewing.
Sherbock, D C and Mantin, R (1994), *Teaching Christianity*, London, Macmillan.
Copley, T (ed.) (1997), *Splashes of God-light*, Swindon, Bible Society.
Fowler, J W, Nipkow, K E and Schweitzer, F (eds) (1992), *Stages of Faith and Reli-
gious Development*, London, SCM.

9. CONTEXT AND PERSPECTIVE

Introduction

This chapter continues questions raised in chapter 8 about the perspective of the reader. In that chapter, the focus was on different religious perspectives and the context of a reader in a particular community of faith. The related focus of this chapter is on readers defined by other circumstances as well, specifically gender, race, economic status and political ideology.

Reflecting on experience

Consider some of your life experiences where being female or male has been significant.

Choose one such experience, and consider how far or how readily someone of the same sex as you, and someone of the opposite sex, could share that experience.

Texts with bias, readers with attitude

If readers have 'vested interests', do the writers of the texts also have a situation and a predisposition which influence the text? The context and perspective of the text, as well as of the reader, are considered in this chapter.

The issues chosen for discussion reflect a confession of faith in Paul's letter to the Galatians 3:26–28, that 'You are all children of God through faith ... There is no longer Jew or Greek ... slave or free ... male and female; for all of you are one in Christ Jesus.' Can there be a fundamental unity in Christ of believers but yet be a difference in the ways people of different identities and life-experiences understand and apply biblical texts?

The Old Testament is read by Palestinian Christians whose ancestors include the Philistines who are displaced by the Israelites who wrote the texts. The New Testament was mainly written by Jewish Christians and yet 'the Jews' are presented in a hostile way by some of the texts. How should the texts be read in the light of these religious/racial perspectives?

The Bible has been used to authorise slavery, racial apartheid and capitalism. It has also been used to justify struggles and rebellion against these political and economic principles and practices. How far is the Bible a handbook for the liberation of the poor and oppressed, or a handbook used to oppress them, or neither of these?

The Bible is read today by individual women and men and to mixed congregations of women and men as if these are texts written equally to both sexes. But were they? Are some of the biblical texts essentially by men and for men? If so, do women and men read and use them differently? We will look at some issues of gender in biblical texts and at the impact of feminist theory and women's experience in Christian use of the Bible.

Ideological analysis

Texts are not objective: the author has a perspective and assumes a perspective (not necessarily the same one) in the readers of the text. A perspective is formed by the beliefs and experiences of a person. Your perspective is your 'view' and, as in purely physical terms, what you see depends on where you stand.

It is a relevant question to ask about a biblical (or any other) text: 'What is the perspective of the author? Where are they standing and consequently what do they see?' This approach is sometimes called an 'ideological' analysis because it attempts to discover the governing beliefs and interests that are contained in texts. The questions are social and political: 'Whose interests are served by this text?', 'What kind of world is envisioned?', 'What roles, duties and values does the text advocate?', 'Whose lifetyle, beliefs and actions does it legitimate?' (see Fiorenza, 1993, p. 4).

An insight from literary analysis is that texts imply a particular type of reader; they have, consciously or unconsciously, a target audience. You, the real reader, may be like that implied person, so you can read the text without having to take on a different attitude from your own. You may be unlike the implied reader, and you may be aware of an attitude or experience which the text assumes in its reader which is not your own. We came across an example of this in chapter 8. The Book of Exodus implies a reader who sides with Moses and with God against the complaining Israelites. Fackenheim wrote that after the experience of the Shoah/Holocaust, a Jewish reader cannot identify with such a person but will identify instead with the perspective of the Israelites.

As in this case, an ideological analysis will examine the interests of the (real) reader as well as of the text. We, the readers, will favour one interpretation over another partly because of our social locations and interests: our gender, race, nation, culture, class, economic status, life experiences. Ideological analysis does not take seriously the commentator who says, 'I am objective. I have no "axe to grind". My reading is neutral in terms of what is valued and advocated in this text.'

Ideological analysis is called 'rhetorical analysis' by some critics (Fiorenza, 1993) because of the recognition that the text is intended to *persuade* the reader to share the perspective and the ideology of the author(s), and that interpreters of texts are also engaging in a rhetorical, persuasive act. In Christian community, of course, preaching and biblical exposition are often explicitly rhetorical, persuasive acts. Persuasive argument is only necessary in a situation where there is more than one possibility of understanding or action, so ideological or rhetorical analysis is particularly conscious of the possibilities of plural meaning in texts.

Jew and Gentile

The Old Testament often reflects the consciousness of a small, beleaguered nation in its exclusions and enmities. Moabites were high on Israel's list of most hated nations and the texts reflect this nationalist/racist hatred, and other exclusions.

EXERCISE
📖 Read Judges 3:15–25.

The satisfaction of the narrator and of the implied reader is clearly enhanced by the obesity of the Moabite king and ▶▶

the circumstance of his being killed while on the lavatory. How far do you identify with that implied reader?

 Read Leviticus 21:16–21.

Racial discrimination is not the only form of discrimination made. The physically disabled were barred from offices of worship.

These are clearly texts with a perspective, a bias. Do we repeat the discriminatory views of the writers when we read the texts, or distance ourselves from the circumstances in which they arose? The racism is not 'unchallenged' by other Old Testament passages: for example, all the nations of the earth are one day to be blessed through the descendants of Abraham (Genesis 12:3). Moreover, remarkably, King David's descent through a Moabite is recorded in the Book of Ruth.

The New Testament was written at a time of controversy of Christian Jews and Christian Gentiles with the Jewish people, and when some Christians were keen to be on good terms with the authority of the Roman empire.

 Read Matthew 27:24–26.

This passage, among others, has had appalling consequences in Christian and Jewish history. Jews, for example, were termed 'deicides', meaning 'killers of God'. It could be argued that the assurance to the Roman empire that its governor was not guilty in the matter of Jesus' death is made at the expense of directing guilt at 'the whole people'.

Probably all of the first Christians and most of the second generation too were Jews, but there is a 'distancing' from Judaism of the followers of Jesus within parts of the Gospels. The Gospel of John uses the phrase 'the Jews' in a distinctive way. '*Iudaioi*' elsewhere can mean either the people of Judea or more broadly the Jewish people as a religious and nationalistic designation, which included the Jews of Galilee for instance. The Gospel of John has both of these uses, but also uses the word as a term for the religious authorities who are hostile to Jesus. For example, in John 9:18–23, two people who are Jews themselves are said to be 'afraid of the Jews'. When Jesus is recorded as saying to 'the Jews' (John 8:44), 'You are from your father the devil, and you choose to do your father's desires', he can be understood as making this accusation only to the powerful religious authorities who opposed him.

In the time of the Gospel (at the end of the first century) the Jews who had accepted Jesus were now simply Christians and members of the church. When Christians in this period spoke of 'Jews', they were referring to those who had rejected Jesus and remained loyal to the synagogue, and who in various ways posed a threat to them, the Christians (Brown, 1971, p. lxxi). (There is an example of the same use in Matthew 28:15.) The 'implied reader' of the Gospel is one who uses the term to describe a hostile group of whose power the reader has reason to be afraid. If our circumstances are different from those of the implied reader, and we repeat this phrase, 'the Jews', as applying to the enemies of Jesus in his own time, we are not making a faithful repetition of the meaning. We are saying something different from what the text meant to the first readers, because to us, the words 'the Jews' mean all or any Jewish people.

EXERCISE

📖 Revisit the two versions of Gospel stories for children in chapter 8. Then find the four uses of 'the Jews' in **John 8:31–59.**

Imagine that on one Sunday you have invited a Jewish friend (who is not a Christian) to attend your church service. You are on the 'rota' to read a Bible passage in the service and it is John 8:31–59. Would you be comfortable reading out a translation which renders *Iudaioi* as 'the Jews'? Could you substitute anything better? How do we stay true to our tradition without *seeming to say* that Jesus, himself a Jew, said all Jews were devilish?

Slave or free

📖 Read Genesis 9:18–27.

The three sons of Noah are seen as the ancestors of three nations or races. The enslavement of Canaanites is justified by this text about their ancestor. The perspective is surely that of those who see themselves as descendants of Shem or Japhet, and not of Ham. This passage was used in the Christian justification of the slavery of black races right up to recent times.

Although there must now be overwhelming agreement within Christian communities that Christian teaching excludes slavery as an acceptable practice, there is also a strong case to be made that various economic structures, not always challenged by the church, can effectively enslave the poor through debt and the threat of starvation. Does the economic context of biblical texts give them a particular perspective on poverty and wealth? Does the economic status or political ideology of you the reader affect your reading of these texts?

There is a story of changing economic pattern discernible in the Old Testament. When Israel ceased to be a semi-nomadic people, it became a nation of farmers and so different social groups with conflicting interests came into being (Boerma, 1979, pp. 10–20). Poverty thereafter was not just seen as a purely material circumstance but could be seen (by the rich) as an indication of inferiority or be experienced (by the poor) as exploitation and oppression. The rich become the target then of much prophetic criticism about unjust conditions (for example, Amos 2:1–6, which was a reading in chapter 3). Social conditions are the subject of seventh-century BCE legislation in the institution of the sabbath year when the produce of the land is to be put at the disposal of the poor, and the year of Jubilee, when all slaves were to be freed and all debts written off (Leviticus 25:1–7, 27). These are radical laws, though it is not clear how far the laws were put into practice, and how far when they were they truly benefited the poor.

At the same time, riches are seen as desirable in many texts, and poverty can be seen as the inevitable outcome of foolishness or idleness. The narrator and implied reader clearly applaud the wealth of the king, for example, when David 'dies in a good old age, full of days, riches and honour' (1 Chronicles 29:28). Wisdom may be better than jewels, but she also promises wealth to those who learn prudence: 'Riches and honour are with me, enduring wealth and prosperity' (Proverbs 8:11, 5 and 18). These texts seem to reflect a different perspective from the one in Amos.

The context of the New Testament texts is not as broad. All share the conditions of the Roman empire with its tension between a wealthy aristocracy and the masses, a relationship described at the time as like that between a wolf and a lamb! In Rome, thousands of unemployed people in Rome lived on a government distribution of grain, the dole. In Judea and Galilee there was a strong feeling of hostility toward the rich ruling class, Jewish landowners who collaborated with Rome. (In the revolt of CE 66, the first act of the rebels in Jerusalem was to burn the city archives with its registers of debts and of land-ownership.) (See Boerma, 1979.)

However, when we investigate the matter of riches and poverty in the New Testament texts, we are still more clearly in the embrace of ideological analysis. Readers differ very widely on how far the references to poverty and wealth relate to social and political organisation and economics. There is a tradition of interpretation that relates texts on wealth and poverty only to individual spiritual qualities, to personal relationships within Christian community, or to eschatological conditions reflecting the final fulfilment of God's purposes (but not the way we get there).

There does seem to be a strain of apolitical (non-political) teaching in the New Testament. Jesus may well have chosen to distinguish his teaching from the Zealots who were the anti-establishment 'activists' in the Judaism of his day. He may have chosen to avoid being identified with expectations of a messiah who would lead the people in a fight for freedom from the tyranny of Rome (John 6:15 may reflect this). This may then be reflected in some of the eschatological ethics of the New Testament which warn the rich of judgement and exhort the poor to be patient for their vindication, but which do not seem to invite them to redress the balance, challenge the oppression or fight for justice.

EXERCISE
  📖 Read the letter of James 5:1–11.

What are the indications that the focus of this teaching is eschatological (remember your work on this in chapter 4) and not a call to political action?

Is the implied reader the 'rich people' of 5:1 or the 'beloved' of 5:7?

📖 Read the letter of James 2:1–9.

Does the letter exhort the reader to action that is social and political, or relational and congregational?

There is a curious tension. Although the letter recommends that people in the Christian 'assembly' be treated impartially with regard neither to their wealth nor to their poverty, the letter ▶▶

itself is not impartial about the actions of the rich as oppressors or the special spiritual status of the poor. (Note that the 'implied reader' is one who is both capable of being oppressed by the rich but also of dishonouring the poor.)

The different context or perspective in particular texts is a factor to take into account.

EXERCISE
📖 **Read Matthew 5:3–11 and Luke 6:20–26.**

Compare the beatitudes (blessings) that Luke lists with the ones from Matthew's list not included in Luke. (They probably had a common source but we do not know if Luke omitted or Matthew added to what was in the source material.) Do you detect an emphasis in Luke that is stronger than in Matthew?

Matthew's 'poor in spirit' is probably not (as it might seem) a diminishing of the idea of material poverty in favour of a spiritualised notion of poverty as humility. It is a Jewish phrase applying to the materially poor. However, Matthew does include the more spiritual notions of meekness and mercy over against Luke's concentration on material conditions (intensified by the matching woes about material conditions).

A superficial assumption about the different contexts of these Gospels would be that Matthew and his readers were wealthy and not concerned to recognise the bias of the Christian proclamation on the side of the poor. It is possible that the reverse is the case. Luke may have been faced with a congregation who were not in material need, or a congregation like the first readers of the letter to James, who needed to be challenged with the blessings for the poor and the woes to the rich. Matthew's congregation may have shared a radical, common poverty (see Matthew 6:24–34) or been more aware of the exploitative power of the rich, making Luke's emphasis not such a necessary one for this congregation.

The context and perspective of the reader has been crucial to the challenge of liberation theology in the twentieth century, developed by and on behalf of the exploited and oppressed of Latin America, Asia and Africa. The liberation of Israel from slavery in Egypt makes the themes of the Exodus central to this theology. It challenges the acceptance of the apolitical strain in the biblical teaching as the right response to the Gospel and to the world we live in. The vehement call for justice in Old Testament prophecy and the radical teaching of Jesus about status (for example, Matthew 25:31–46) are seen as governing themes for Christian theology. An eschatological interpretation that has required 2,000 years of patient suffering from the poor is rejected.

There is a particular insistence in liberation theology on the relationship of biblical interpretation and experience. Experience, and integration of the Bible with the world, was noted as essential for Christian biblical interpretation in chapter 8. Liberation theology notes that the human experience that has governed the church's traditions of biblical interpretation has been that of affluent, white, male, western academics and church dignitaries. It has also been a tradition that theorises, and whose interpretations can be historical or literary or theological in ways that do not translate into action. Itumelong Mosala argues that by removing the text from experience and practice, western interpreters screen out the 'sighs and groans for freedom and dignity' (Brueggemann, 1997, p. 101) expressed in the text, and that by doing so they (perhaps that should be 'we') construct a racist interpretation. The church must take sides with the poor, join with their cry for deliverance, and read the Bible from within that context and with that perspective.

Some liberation theologians argue that the bias of a biblical text can make it unusable in the struggle for liberation. If a text has been written with an oppressive perspective, for example, Genesis 9:18–27, with its apparent intention to justify the subjugation and slavery of the other nations, then it will continue to convey an exploitative message. The only use of such a text must be to help to expose the oppressive nature of some biblical texts and of their interpretation in a church which represents the interests of the élite rather than those of oppressed people.

EXERCISE

In this tradition of biblical interpretation, the context of the interpreter is the keystone. The exodus theme has the liberation of the Hebrews at one end, but at the other the slaughter and enslavement of the inhabitants of Canaan by the Hebrews.

📖 Read Exodus 2:23–25 and Joshua 8:1–2.　　　　▶▶

> How far are you able to share the perspective of the narrator and the implied reader in both cases, that of the oppressed and the oppressor?

Critics of liberation theology ask why one aspect of the exodus theme should be seen as more authoritative than the other. Liberation theologians reply by focusing on the context of the reader: if the reader shares the context of the poor and the oppressed, there will be no doubt about which is the aspect that is relevant and authoritative (Barr, 1993b, p. 601). The authority comes from the context.

Male and female

There are clear parallels between responses to the Bible and biblical interpretation from the poor and from liberation theology to responses from women readers and from feminist theologies. In each case there is a consciousness of the context and perspective of the text and the context and perspective of the reader.

There are many different approaches to biblical interpretation within this consciousness, however. Some, in the same way as some liberation theologians, reject particular texts as oppressive and unusable: the texts describe women as inferior and subordinate, and describe and perpetuate the abuse of women (some examples will be given below).

Others, again like some liberation theologians, argue that it is not the texts that are oppressive to women but the tradition of interpreting them. Feminist theology can be seen as a prophetic movement in the church, pronouncing judgement and calling for repentance.

EXERCISE

There is a striking illustration of a tradition of interpretation that is more discriminatory against women than, arguably, the biblical text it interprets. Recall (without looking up the Bible passage yet: you read it for chapter 7) the story in Genesis of the woman and the serpent in the Garden of Eden. In many paintings of this, and in the medieval mystery cycle plays about it, and in Milton's *Paradise Lost*, the woman is tempted by the serpent, eats some of the fruit, and then goes to find the man who has been asleep or ▶▶

> somewhere else in the garden. She tempts or seduces the man and
> he eats the fruit.
>
> 📖 **Read Genesis 3:1–13 again.**
>
> Is that what the text says?

Some people who think they know the Bible well can be surprised to
find that the story says that the man was present all the time (verse 6).
The man certainly blames the woman when God confronts him, and the
tradition of interpretation has agreed with him! It is an interpretation
that is reflected in the New Testament itself. In 1 Timothy 2:14 the
author says, 'Adam was not deceived, but the woman was deceived and
became a transgressor.' This New Testament text makes this a reason
why a woman is to be subordinate to a man.

Another approach is one that accepts that the context of the texts,
written largely by men and for men, is one of discrimination against
women, but it takes the perspective of a woman reader looking for positive insights in the texts. This approach finds that there are characters
and themes within the Bible which run counter to the prevailing male-
centred culture.

📖 **Read Genesis 1:27.** The reader reads this before the story of
Genesis 3, which may or may not blame the woman for deceiving
the man, and before the story of Genesis 2, which says the man was
created first and alone. In spite of the prevailing view in the later
stories of woman as perverse and subordinate, the reader starts off
with the insight that humankind was created as male and female,
and that this creation reflects the image of God. God then is neither
male nor female, and the woman no less than the man is made in
God's image and likeness. If the Bible is male-centred it also,
arguably, counters its own male-centred perspective.

This 'against-the-grain' perspective does not eliminate the male bias
of scripture or neglect the evidence of the discriminatory texts. Phyllis
Trible calls it a 'remnant' (Trible, 1990). 'Remnant theology' reflects the
prophetic tradition of the exile where the people of God have been
destroyed but a remnant of the people who survive or return will be a
sign of hope of the promise of God to all the people.

Some texts are so abusive of the women in them that it is hard to use them in such a theology of hope, other than to call to remembrance the suffering of such women. There is Tamar (Genesis 38), refused a husband by Judah and condemned for being pregnant with his child; Dinah, Leah's daughter (Genesis 34), raped by a Hivite and then wanted for his wife, whose brothers then take revenge on men, women and children; the unnamed woman of Judges 19, handed to a mob by her man to protect himself, raped and abused by the mob for the course of the night, and then cut into pieces by her man. There are some terrible stories in the Bible, to which an easy response is surely inappropriate.

The New Testament presents a very interesting context where, it seems, women may have found a much more equal role, perhaps among the first followers of Jesus, and perhaps in some of the first churches, particularly Paul's. Paul's letters suggest that women exercised charismatic ministries like prayer and prophecy, and several women are listed as fellow workers, evangelists, teachers, benefactors. Junia, for example (Romans 16:7), is an apostle. It is clear from later letters in the post-Pauline tradition (like 1 Timothy of which one verse was quoted above) that if there was such an early equality it did not continue even through the first century: women are quickly excluded from roles of authority in these churches. John's Gospel may reflect, right at the end of the century, one Christian community which held on to an understanding of women and men in an equal discipleship. The Samaritan woman (4:7–42), Martha (11:27) and Mary Magdalene (20:17–18) make confessions and undertake missions that suggest this.

In all these examples, the perspective, bias and presuppositions of the reader make a great difference to how any text is interpreted. Consider the further example of how the Bible is used by evangelical Christians in debates on the roles of women in the church (Noll, 1991, p. 207). Those who believe that the Bible gives God's detailed instruction for human behaviour, and that western society is degenerate, tend to be convinced by interpretations of biblical texts that reinforce a pattern of subordinate female roles. On the other hand, those who believe that the purpose of the Bible is God's on-going revelation to humanity, and that developments in society are sometimes instructive to Christians, tend to be convinced by interpretations that suggest or allow for a wide scope of women's authority. 'What you see depends on where you stand.'

The absence or silence of women in so many of the biblical texts, and their subordinate or abusive treatment in some, has led to a particular use of the strategy called in chapter 3 'reading the gaps'. Retellings of these stories from the perspective of the women in the texts could be said to give these women a voice. It might also be argued that these retellings are 'merely fiction', acts of the imagination, while the biblical version is inspired scripture. ('What you see depends …')

EXERCISE
📖 Read Exodus 1:1 to 2:10 and 15:20–21.

This could be seen as one of those texts that work 'against the grain' of male-centred scripture and male-dominant interpretation. There is an extraordinary solidarity of women in resisting the oppressor (Watson, 1994, pp. 195–200). Shiphrah, Puah, Jochebed (Moses' mother: see Exodus 6:20), Miriam, Pharaoh's daughter and her female servants, together preserve the life of a child and if they had not, Moses could not have led the people of God out of slavery to the land of promise. Miriam's song of triumph (15:20–21) when the liberation is accomplished can remind the reader of her participation as a child in the women's resistance at the outset, which brought about this triumph.

Consider now the selection of a Church of England lectionary in setting this story for reading in worship and look at who has been cut out: **Exodus 1:1–14, 22 to 2:10.**

What is it in the context of Christian worship or in the perspective of those who select these readings that might lead to the exclusion of the role of Shiphrah and Puah as saviours of their people? Is it a perspective you share or seek to challenge?

Further reading

Bauckham, R (1989), *The Bible in Politics*, London, SPCK.
Clines, D J A, Fowl, S E and Porter, S E (eds) (1990), *The Bible in Three Dimensions*, Sheffield, JSOT Press.
Dennis, T (1993), *Sarah Laughed: women's voices in the Old Testament*, London, SPCK.
Day, P L, Gottwald, N K, Jobling, D and Sheppard, G T (1991), *The Bible and the Politics of Exegesis*, London, Darton, Longman and Todd.
Loades, A (ed.) (1990), *Feminist Theology: a reader*, London, SPCK.
Newsom, C A and Ringe, S H (eds) (1992), *The Women's Bible Commentary*, London, SPCK.
Maitland, S (1993), *Daughter of Jerusalem*, London, Virago (the ends of each chapter).
Pixley, J and Boff, C (1989), *The Bible, the Church and the Poor*, London, Burns and Oates.

10. APPLYING THE SKILLS

Introduction

This chapter is intended as a consolidation of some of the material and methods you have been investigating. Instead of taking examples from many different biblical texts, here our focus will be on just one, and we will apply to the text some of the skills that have been discussed and illustrated in preceding chapters. This will also give us an opportunity to see how far the different methods may be used together on the same text.

> ### Reflecting on experience
> You have now had experience of a range of approaches to biblical texts, including those in the preceding chapters.
>
> Looking back over the book, which approaches or examples have you found most and least interesting, useful or congenial to your own ways of thinking?

Historical-critical exegesis and other approaches

In chapters 2 and 8, it was recognised that the predominant methods of interpreting text in the Christian tradition have been those concerned with historical issues. The underlying questions addressed by historical criticism of the Gospels are 'What do the Gospels tell us about Jesus and about the communities or churches for which the individual Gospels were written?' These are the questions that most biblical commentaries on the Gospels investigate. The approach tends to be 'author-centred' (see chapter 2): the meaning of the text that is sought is primarily the meaning intended by the author to the first readers of it. This type of interpretation is often called 'exegesis' which means just 'interpretation' but is used by many as a shorthand for 'historical-critical exegesis'.

The historical skills discussed in chapter 6 are obviously central to this type of exegesis. So are the textual matters referred to in chapter 2. Translation (chapters 2 and 5) is interpretation too and many commentaries will discuss how best to translate a particular text or word.

Are the other skills and approaches we have looked at a part of historical-critical exegesis? The answer might differ from one commentator to another. Some of the linguistic and literary skills (chapters 5 and 7) of any reading cannot be separated from historical-critical exegesis. Metaphors, structure, characters and plot are part of how the authors have expressed their intention and part of the way we apprehend it. There are literary methods where historical issues are *not* the concern: 'synchronic' methods (see chapter 7) which have barely figured in this book.

Similarly, the religious and political perspectives (chapters 8 and 9) are just as hard to disentangle from historical methods. Proponents of ideological or rhetorical analysis (chapter 9) argue that it is not possible to have a scientifically objective reading of a text, unaffected by the commentator's perspective. Both historical-critical exegesis and ideological analysis can nevertheless analyse text and context with accuracy and critical rigour. If socio-historical investigation discovers issues in the text that relate to economic, cultural and political situations, does that give us an historical interpretation or a political one? Perhaps we do not have to make such categorical distinctions.

The religious perspectives are not less 'ideological' than political ones and as we saw they too usually share the concern for historical issues. Redaction criticism is a tool that sees the text as part of an historical process (the Evangelist has selected and edited stories and sayings passed down in oral or written form) but redaction critics are interested in the *theological* purposes that guided this selection and expression. If we find, say, a theology of discipleship in the Gospel of Mark, is that historical-critical exegesis or Christian interpretation? Again, it may possibly be both.

📖 **Read Mark 1:14_31.**

An exegesis always begins with a careful reading of the passage and, if necessary, a re-reading of the whole book from which the passage is taken.

The text chosen is a series of verses from near the beginning of the

Gospel according to Mark. The *New Revised Standard Version* text is printed as a column within the chart that follows. This is the 'final form' of the text that will be used, though other translations or the Greek text itself could also be referred to. You are recommended to study the passage in any modern translation you are accustomed to use *as well* as this translation. The comparison may be useful. (You may choose to revisit the notes about different translations in chapter 1 to see why the *New Revised Standard Version* might be one of the preferred versions for exegesis.)

A standard academic exegesis includes investigations using the textual, literary, historical, socio-historical and theological skills described. They would not usually be divided into these sections. In order to relate different findings in the text to the different methods this book has described, this chapter demonstrates a halfway stage, not a finished exegesis. The final stage would take the material from the chart and the different sections below and arrange it in paragraphs structured on the different sections or verses and on different themes rather than the different methods of analysis. How far all the material from Christian theological interpretation and from political and feminist perspectives can be or should be part of an historical-critical exegesis is a matter of personal judgement.

The text

The NRSV text of Mark 1:14–31 is printed here for your convenience.

[14] Now after John was arrested, Jesus came to Galilee, proclaiming the good news of God[h], [15] and saying, 'The time is fulfilled, and the kingdom of God has come near;[i] repent, and believe in the good news.'

[16] As Jesus passed along the Sea of Galilee, he saw Simon and his brother Andrew casting a net into the lake – for they were fishermen. [17] And Jesus said to them, 'Follow me and I will make you fish for people.' [18] And immediately they left their nets and followed him. [19] As he went a little farther, he saw James son of Zebedee and his brother John, who were in their boat mending the nets. [20] Immediately he called them; and they left their father Zebedee in the boat with the hired men, and followed him.

[21] They went to Capernaum; and when the sabbath came, he

entered the synagogue and taught. [22]They were astounded at his teaching, for he taught them as one having authority, and not as the scribes. [23] Just then there was in their synagogue a man with an unclean spirit, [24] and he cried out, 'What have you to do with us, Jesus of Nazareth? Have you come to destroy us? I know who you are, the Holy One of God.' [25] But Jesus rebuked him, saying, 'Be silent, and come out of him!' [26] And the unclean spirit, throwing him into convulsions and crying with a loud voice, came out of him. [27] They were all amazed, and they kept on asking one another, 'What is this? A new teaching – with authority! He*j* commands even the unclean spirits, and they obey him.' [28] At once his fame began to spread throughout the surrounding region of Galilee.

[29] As soon as they*k* left the synagogue, they entered the house of Simon and Andrew, with James and John. [30] Now Simon's mother-in-law was in bed with a fever, and they told him about her at once. [31] He came and took her by the hand and lifted her up. Then the fever left her, and she began to serve them.

---

h *Other ancient authorities read* of the kingdom
i *Or* is at hand
j *Or* A new teaching! With authority he
k *Other ancient authorities read* he

Textual skills

The *New Revised Standard Version* footnotes tell us there are two manuscript variations ('other ancient authorities read …') in our passage that might be significant, and two questions of translation ('or …'). We examined similar instances in chapter 2. The commentaries can guide us as to whether these should affect our interpretation. The only one that seems really significant is the decision to translate 1:14 as 'the kingdom of God has come near' or 'the kingdom of God is at hand'. Scholars take different views (see Hooker, 1991, pp. 54f) as to whether the Greek verb here should be read as meaning 'approaching' (not here yet) or 'arriving' (here already). Is the eschatology of Mark's Gospel an imminent eschatology (the end is coming but not here) or realised (the end is a reality not just an expectation)? The term 'inaugurated' (begun but not complete) might best describe this eschatology (Fuller, 1954, pp. 21–25). Because the phrase in Mark is in Greek, and Jesus' own proclamation was probably in Aramaic, the question of whether Jesus' own eschatology was imminent, realised or inaugurated is a separate one, not based on this linguistic question.

Literary skills

The *New Revised Standard Version* paragraphs (the Greek manuscripts have no paragraph divisions and no chapter or verse numbers) suggest four episodes, which most readers would distinguish, namely verses 14–15, 16–20, 21–28 and 29–31. Using first the standard literary skills of a reader, we analyse the text in terms of sequence of episodes and themes, settings (time and place), characters and plot. If we have read the whole of Mark's Gospel carefully, and if we know or look up in a Bible dictionary what particular culture-specific words mean (synagogue, sabbath, scribe, etc.), we can get a long way towards our exegesis, before we open the commentaries.

EXERCISE

Some people find it helpful to document material like this in a chart (see the chart in Myers, Dennis, Nangle, Moe-Lobeda and Taylor, 1996, pp. 213ff). You will need a large sheet of paper ruled into five columns:

The text	Sequence of episodes and themes	Setting: time and place	Character	Plot

and the rows will be the different sections, verses 14–15, 16–20, 21–28 and 29–31. One strategy for the first column is to make an enlarged photocopy of the text, cut out the sections and paste these in.

You then need to fill in the grid with notes based on your own reading of the text, under the headings. This gives you a visual aid to understand the connection of one passage with the next, recurring themes, the movement of the narrative from one setting to another or from some main characters to others.

The notes below may illustrate the sort of findings that you could put into such a grid, not drawn from commentaries but from reading the text with the narrative skills of a careful reader.

Mark 1:14–15
Sequence
- Verses 14 and 15 are the culmination of the prologue to Mark's Gospel: Jesus' presence and ministry has been prepared for by John the Baptist's ministry, and Jesus himself has prepared for it in baptism and a time in the wilderness.
- The summary of Jesus' message stands as a heading to all that follows.

Setting
- There is a transition from Judea to Galilee, the general setting of the first half of Jesus' ministry in Mark's Gospel. The time follows the ministry of John the Baptist.
- The Kingdom of God is a metaphorical, eschatological 'place' that is announced as close or present. An eschatological 'time' begins now or soon.

Characters
- John the Baptist has been the forerunner (1:4) to the main character Jesus.
- God's presence is imminent in the Reign or Kingdom.
- Herod is implied by the arrest but does not appear until 6:14.

Plot
- Jesus preaches repentance and so fulfils the expectation (1:7) of a successor to John. An eschatological 'plot' is begun and the expectation of the coming Kingdom and the end 'time': a new story is about to begin.
- This 'time' also fulfils an older expectation (OT promises).

Mark 1:16–20
Sequence
- Repentance (1:15) may be an idea that links the episodes: it means a 'turning about' like the change of life the fishermen make. In Mark 8:34 followers must 'deny themselves' and Peter reminds Jesus (10:28) that they have.
- John the Baptist in Judea had had a large following (1:5): four men now follow Jesus.
- The theme of discipleship runs right through Mark's Gospel.

Setting
- From the general 'Galilee' there is a more specific location to two sites along the shore of the Sea of Galilee.

• There is no direct time sequence between this episode and the last. It is nevertheless presented as the first action of Jesus apart from his preaching.

Characters
• Verses 1–15 featured John the Baptist and Jesus. Now Jesus remains and the new characters, Jesus' disciples, join him for the rest of the narrative (though male disciples are absent during the crucifixion).

Plot
• The expectation of the fulfilment of the 'time' (1:15) and the coming 'Kingdom' is taken a step further with the enlisting of workers for one of the tasks of the end-time (1:17).
• The response of the disciples 'immediately' (a favourite word of Mark's) reflects the urgency of 1:15.
• They follow him: the expectation is 'Where? To do what?'

Mark 1:21–28
Sequence
• The call to discipleship of a few is followed by public teaching to many.
• The clashes with the scribes, implicit here, is explicit through the narrative, culminating first in 3:6 and finally in the trial before the Sanhedrin.
• The episode climaxes in 'the spread of his fame' (cf. John the Baptist in 1:5) and will be followed through in the insistence Jesus makes on moving on to preach (1:37–39).

Setting
• The location and time are specific: sabbath in the Capernaum synagogue (the Jewish institutions of synagogue, sabbath law and the scribes appear for the first time).
• The 'surrounding region of Galilee' (1:28) remains a centre of operation until 10:1.

Characters
• Jesus is accompanied now by his four disciples.
• The people in the synagogue ('They', 1:22) react: they are the seed of a growing crowd of witnesses (1:28). A group is mentioned, the scribes, who do not speak or act until later (2:6).

- A man with an unclean spirit and the unclean spirit are the first of a succession of similar characters/roles.
- An opposition between Jesus and such spirits is made explicit – the 'Holy One' against the 'unclean' – first hinted at in 1:13.

Plot
- Jesus continues to be depicted as taking prompt and assertive action (1:21). His authority and his exorcism may in part fulfil the promise of the coming Kingdom (1:15).
- The man's/spirit's questions, 'What have you to do with us? Have you come to destroy us?' and the people's question, 'What is this (teaching/authority)?' is a question set up for Mark's Gospel to answer, beyond this episode.
- Jesus' spreading fame sets up an expectation of public, perhaps official response.

Mark 1:29–31
Sequence
- The scene is 'typical' of healings in Mark's Gospel.
- There are other women disciples who 'serve' Jesus in 15:41.

Setting
- There is an 'immediate' move from a public to a private location of Simon and Andrew's house in Capernaum. This seems to become the headquarters (2:1).
- The time is still the sabbath (see 1:32).

Characters
- Simon, Andrew, James and John are all named again. Jesus remains the central character.
- Simon's mother-in-law is the first individual woman mentioned in the narrative.

Plot
- After the first exorcism, there is the first healing – the first of many of both (1:32–34): again are these meant as signs of the arrival of the Kingdom?
- The woman's action suggests that it is (see 10:42–45).

EXERCISE

The next stage is to examine your findings and make connections or note things that puzzle you, for further investigation. Read your chart vertically as well as horizontally, to examine the developments or sequences. Don't forget to go back to the text itself and read the whole thing through again, alert to what your literary analysis has helped you recognise.

These literary skills are particularly essential in an exegesis to establish the context of a text (its relationship to the immediately preceding and succeeding material and its place and function in the whole Gospel).

The analysis also gives you an indication of the issues in the text you should certainly comment on, for example, Christology, eschatology, discipleship (see under theological interpretation). If these or other issues emerge that you feel you need more information about, then you know what to look for in the commentaries or other resources like Bible dictionaries.

Historical skills

Our exegesis is 'historical-critical' in its concern for what the Gospel tells us about Jesus and about the Markan community, and 'author-centred' in its search for the meaning of the text intended by the author to the first readers of it. (We do not know the name of the author of the Gospel, other than through the later tradition that calls him Mark.) If we accept the 'two-document hypothesis' (see chapter 6) our understanding of the *sources* of this Gospel and the *form* of units of tradition that Mark used is largely guesswork. It is *redaction* criticism that is a key method, in relation to our guesses about the source and form of the material.

Parallels to Mark's material in Luke or Matthew (to which the commentaries, or Gospel parallels, can alert you) that seem to draw on independent sources may help us with questions of Mark's sources. Was the whole of 1:16–20 a unit of tradition that Mark received? This is probable. Andrew is not prominent in the rest of Mark's Gospel as Peter, James and John are, and Luke 5:1–11 shows that an Evangelist could record a call to Peter without reference to Andrew (Best, 1981, p. 166), and so it is unlikely that Mark would have added Andrew to a unit of tradition about the call of Peter. Similarly (redaction criticism) if it was Mark who made up the phrase 'fishers of people' we would expect him to use the idea later in the Gospel too and he does not. However, might Mark have constructed 1:19–20 and added it to the tradition about Andrew and Peter? James and John are included, and called to follow, in Luke 5:1–11 (comparing sources again), but not as a separate incident. On balance (redaction criticism) it seems more likely that this was a tradition that came to Mark rather than an episode constructed by him, because his Gospel does not seek to elevate James and John among the disciples. Indeed, in 10:39–40 they are rebuked for pretensions to elevation (Best, 1981, p. 167). Mark's hand is evident in the editing (redaction) of the unit, though: 'and immediately' (1:18) is a characteristic phrase of his.

Although we do not know for certain what sources Mark had available, the consensus of scholarship is not that he used every scrap of material known to him but that he chose what to include, and chose how to arrange it, because he considered that this made an important and relevant message to the people for whom he wrote. Older commentators would not have agreed: for example, according to Hengel (1985, p. 34) it was Bultmann's view in 1963 that

> Mark is not sufficiently master of his material to be able to venture on a systematic construction himself.

The decision to juxtapose the proclamation of Jesus (1:15) with the end of John the Baptist's ministry was probably Mark's (see chapter 6). It was probably also Mark's decision that heads the Gospel with the summary of Jesus' proclamation, and follows it with a call to discipleship and then with an episode that demonstrates people's reaction to the authority Jesus showed in teaching and exorcism, and that follows that with a particular series of healings beginning with Peter's mother-in-law. It is the authority of Jesus that impresses the reader in this presentation of the material. According to Hooker (1991, p. 53):

> Here is a religious teacher, healer and leader who comes from outside the system, apparently without credentials, and yet preaches with tremendous effect. It is hardly surprising if ordinary people ask one another, 'What is this?' (1:27) or if the religious authorities are resentful and indignant.

(Redaction criticism shares such findings with literary criticism.)

In 1:24, the unclean spirit declares that it knows who Jesus is, and in 1:25 Jesus commands silence about his person or his work. A similar thing happens repeatedly in Mark's Gospel, and it is a matter raising literary, historical and theological questions. A scholar called Wrede first explained this, the 'messianic secret', as a device to explain why Jesus was not acknowledged as Messiah during his ministry. He argued that the interpretation of Jesus' words, actions and role as messianic was unhistorical. Many scholars disagree since it is reasonably certain that Jesus was put to death as a messianic pretender (Mark 14:61; 15:26) (Hooker 1991, p. 67). Some scholars (Taylor, Cranfield) argued against Wrede that the 'messianic secret' was historical: Jesus wished to conceal his messiahship for fear that it would be misunderstood as a claim to political kingship, and his favoured title for himself was the more ambiguous 'Son of Man'. There are two problems with this view: it means that Jesus leaves his disciples confused about his own understanding of his messiahship and that he tells people to be silent about things which it seems unreasonable to expect them to keep silent, for example, the restoration to life of a child (5:43). A third explanation is that the commands to secrecy are largely (not necessarily entirely) introduced by Mark as a literary device to draw the reader's attention to the theological meaning of his story. The truth remains hidden from bystanders, from the religious authorities and even, before the resurrection, remains partly hidden from the disciples themselves, because it is something intelligible only to those who believe that Jesus is what these voices declare him to be. The 'secret' is an open secret to the reader. This may have a basis in history as well as being a literary device. Jesus may have been reluctant to make specific claims about himself. According to Hooker (1991, p. 69):

> Artificial though the secret may be, there is a sense in which it corresponds to the truth about the way in which Jesus came to be acknowledged as Messiah only through suffering and death.

Socio-historical investigation

One of the major contributions of the commentaries is information that may not be apparent from the text itself but which research into geographical, social, religious or economic factors suggests is relevant to our understanding of the meaning of the text.

The religious status of Galilee, for example, may form part of Mark's message. The location of John the Baptist in the wilderness and in Judea conforms to a pattern of messianic expectation: by proclaiming the good news in Galilee, Jesus is shown to be challenging such expectations (Hooker, 1991, p. 54). Away from the religious centre of Jerusalem, Jesus proclaims the good news of God in semi-pagan Galilee. (See also political perspectives below.)

Jesus' actions in the synagogue need to be understood in relation to Jewish religious tradition of the time. According to Anderson (1976, pp. 89f):

> Any adult male Israelite, especially if he enjoyed the reputation of being skilled in interpretation of the Law and scribal tradition, could be invited to preach. The Gospel tradition depicts Jesus as having free access to the synagogue and suggests that he was recognised as a rabbi ... Whether he was officially trained as such we do not know. (Anderson, 1976, p. 89f)

More than one view can be taken of the information we unearth. Nineham argues that the teaching of the scribes was not at this time necessarily derivative and dependent on their predecessors. Nineham (1992, pp. 74f) suggests that

> properly ordained rabbis with full rabbinic authority seldom penetrated to Galilee and the Galileans were therefore amazed.

This reflects an interest in the historical tradition underlying the Gospel: Nineham acknowledges that even if this is the case, this is not Mark's point (redaction criticism).

Miracle-working and exorcism are also matters for investigation: for example, the words used in 1:25, 'rebuked' and 'Be silent' are both terms used in the ancient world as formulas for exorcism (Nineham, 1992, p. 75). That Mark is revealing Jesus as something more than a miracle-worker is clear from the words of the unclean spirit.

Theological interpretation

Christian theology and Christian readers have a particular interest in the Christology and the eschatology of the passage and in Mark's message about discipleship. Christian theology understands the Gospel to be not only proclaimed by Jesus (Mark 1:15) but to be about him: for Christians, 'Jesus is the Gospel and the Gospel is Jesus' (Barrett, 1955, p. 58). This understanding sees the eschatological Kingdom or sovereignty of God announced by Jesus to be made present by him and in him.

Christology is the key interpretative factor for everything else (eschatology, discipleship, etc.) in the text.

The historical and religious context in which Jesus speaks and Mark writes includes the idea from the Old Testament of the kingship of God, and the hope of a time when God would defeat rebellion and the nations would be obedient to Israel's God (for example, Isaiah 24:23). When Mark shows Jesus announcing this reign of God as having 'come near' and then shows him recruiting disciples to participate in the judgement of the end-time (the fishing metaphor, Mark 1:17), teaching with authority from God, exorcising rebellious spirits and healing the poor and outcast, he is demonstrating the presence of God's reign in what Jesus says and does.

At least some in Mark's (and Jesus') time believed that the reign of God relied on the political and military intervention of the Messiah (Myers, 1988, p. 135). Malachi 3:1 was understood to promise such intervention. Jesus (and Mark) may have had to defeat and adjust such expectations. Christian interpretation has tended to downplay the social and political reality of God's reign in Jesus' proclamation, and Mark's Gospel, in favour of a Christology of personal relationship. Schweizer (1971, pp. 46f) wrote:

> To Judaism the Kingdom of God was far more important than the Messiah, whereas here everything depends on the fellowship with Jesus. In Judaism the world was expected to be either transfigured or destroyed in the fire of judgement, whereas this saying of Jesus (1:15) placed his disciples and their duties in the midst of the world. At the same time, however, it makes them inwardly free from the world and, as a consequence, the world is neither condemned nor exalted. Jesus, therefore, has no expectation of the triumph of Israel or of the church, and the condemnation of everyone else. To a disciple of Jesus, what God's judgement says to him (or her) is the only essential.

(This is a thoroughly non-political reading – see below.)

The personal qualities of Jesus (not described by Mark but, arguably, implied in the responses of the people) are often made the subject of commentary in Christian tradition: so, according to Lane (1974, p. 58), the action of Peter's mother-in-law:

> confirms the mercy and compassion extended toward her by Jesus and indicates that the figures in the background of the Gospel narrative are affected by the power of this mysterious Galilean.

Political perspectives

By contrast Ched Myers, in a groundbreaking commentary on the Gospel of Mark, gives a reading of the Gospel informed by socio-historical investigation of the context of the Gospel (which he locates at the time of the Jewish rebellion in the late 60s CE and among the peasants of Galilee) and by his own perspective of Christian belief and use of Marxist theory. He detects three plot strands and three key aspects to Jesus' messianic programme and his proclamation of the Kingdom of God (Mark 1:15): confronting the old order, constructing an alternative order and bringing liberation to the poor (Myers, 1988, p. 121).

Myers (1988, p. 132) considers that the old order is challenged in the fishing metaphor of Mark 1:16–20.

> There is perhaps no expression more traditionally misunderstood than Jesus' invitation to these workers to become 'fishers of men', usually taken to mean 'the saving of souls'.

In the Old Testament, the hooking of fish is a euphemism for judgement upon the rich (for example, Amos 4:2) and the powerful (for example, Ezekiel 29:4). Mark's Jesus is inviting common folk to join him in his struggle to overturn the existing order of power and privilege. Myers notes the tendency of commentators to deny that this call, to radical abandonment of the socio-economic order, is the pattern for all discipleship of Jesus: they opt for a 'bourgeois' interpretation that this radical call can be explained away by Jesus' expectation of an imminent end of the world.

According to Myers (1988, p. 137), conflict about authority in Mark 1:21–22 and Mark 1:27 frames the exorcism story, 1:23–26.

> From the moment he strides into a Capernaum synagogue, it becomes clear that Jesus' kingdom project is incompatible with the local public authorities and the social order they represent.

Myers (1988, p. 142) argues that this framing structure suggests that the reader is meant to understand the exorcism as related to the struggle between the authority of Jesus and that of the scribes. When the unclean spirit asks, 'Have you come to destroy *us*?', it is pleading on behalf of the group already identified in the conflict theme, the scribes, the upholders of the order Jesus will destroy.

The next episode, Mark 1:29–31, illustrates the socio-economic bias in the traditions of Jesus' miracles. Theissen (in Myers, 1988, p. 144) considers that the miracle stories focus on:

> specific situations of distress, on possession, disease, hunger, lack of success, and danger, in other words on situations which do not strike as hard in all social groups ... It seems to me that a degree of class correlation in the primitive Christian miracle stories can hardly be denied.

Feminist perspectives

The perspective that sees Mark's Gospel as describing Jesus' challenge to the existing order of power and privilege is shared by those who see the challenge as including the challenge to the order of male power enshrined in patriarchy. The shift of location from synagogue to a private home in Mark 1:29 is a pattern reflected throughout the Gospel: it seems (Myers, Dennis, Nangle, Moe-Lobeda and Taylor, 1996, pp. 14f) that Mark contrasts the synagogue and Temple as places of political conflict with the home as a safe site: 'a depiction that no doubt reflects the experience of the early church.' Women were able to speak, act and interact in the home environment in a way that most were unable to do in public.

A common older pattern of commentary on Mark 1:29–31 refers to the tradition that Mark wrote down Simon Peter's version of these events; this is counted as sufficient to explain why this episode of Simon's home-life is included. The service which the woman offers to Jesus and the (male) disciples is then seen as the usual domestic role of women in patriarchal households. Schweizer (1971, p. 53), indeed, holds it to be the role of women in the church too: 'The story concludes with an act of service which is the specific manner of discipleship for a woman.'

📖 Read Mark 10:35–45 and 15:40–41.

The verb 'to serve' that is used occurs only two other times in the Gospel. In 10:45, Jesus uses it about his own saving ministry as part of his rebuke to the (male) disciples and in contrast to the established structures of dominance. In 15:41 (translated in the *New Revised Standard Version* as 'provided for') it is used again of women, in conjunction with the phrase 'followed him' which signifies discipleship (male as well as female) in this Gospel. Myers, Dennis, Nangle, Moe-Lobeda and Taylor (1996, p. 15) argue that:

> In other words, both at the outset and at the conclusion of Mark's Gospel, women, in a society which devalued them, are identified as the true disciples. In this 'minor' healing, Mark is serving notice that patriarchal theology and the devaluation of women will be overturned!

Contrast this view with Schweizer's above, which takes no account of this verb as a characteristic of Jesus.

EXERCISES

It might now be helpful to return to some of the exercises you undertook earlier and revisit your responses in the light of your further studies. For example, revisit the questions about right and wrong interpretations of biblical texts in chapter 1, about the possibilities of more than one meaning in a text at the end of chapter 2, and about the priority of historical-critical interpretation at the end of chapter 6.

Try also some more ambitious exercises than those suggested so far, to consolidate and develop your skills and understanding. Two are suggested here:

Write an exegesis of a short biblical passage (for example, Mark 1:1–15; Mark 2:1–11; John 2:1–12) using a good selection of resources: at least three commentaries, with Bible dictionaries, etc. See the suggestions for further reading below, but also find recent scholarly commentaries on the particular book of the Bible.

Research and write an essay on the interpretation of a short biblical passage according to one or more of the perspectives outlined in the previous chapters (for example, traditional and feminist interpretations of Genesis 2:7 and 18–25, or of Genesis 3:1–20; Jewish and Christian interpretation of Isaiah 53; literary and political analysis of Luke 1:39–56; or theological and political analysis of Luke 1:39–56.

Further reading

Coggins, R J and Houlden, J L (eds) (1990), *A Dictionary of Biblical Interpretation*, London, SCM.

Fee, G D (1993), *New Testament Exegesis: a handbook for students and pastors*, Louisville, Kentucky, Westminster John Knox Press.

Green, J B, McKnight, S and Howard-Marshall, I (eds) (1992), *Dictionary of Jesus and the Gospels*, Downers Grove, Illinois, IVP.

Hayes, J H and Holladay, C R (1988), *Biblical Exegesis: a beginner's handbook*, London, SCM.

Hooker, M D (1983), *The Message of Mark*, London, Epworth Press.

Hooker, M D (1991), *A Commentary on the Gospel according to St Mark*, London, A and C Black.

Myers, C (1988), *Binding the Strong Man: a political reading of Mark's story of Jesus*, Maryknoll, New York, Orbis.

Myers, C, Dennis, M, Nangle, J, Moe-Lobeda, C and Taylor, S (1996), *Say to this Mountain: Mark's story of discipleship*, Maryknoll, New York, Orbis.

Stenger, W (1993), *Introduction to NT Exegesis*, Grand Rapids, Michigan, Eerdmans.

REFERENCES

Alexander, P S (1993), Interpretation, history of: Jewish interpretation, in B M Metzger and M D Coogan (eds), *The Oxford Companion to the Bible*, Oxford, Oxford University Press.

Anderson, H (1976), *The Gospel of Mark*, London, Marshall, Morgan and Scott.

Barr, J (1993a), Interpretation, history of: modern biblical criticism, in B M Metzger and M D Coogan (eds), *The Oxford Companion to the Bible*, Oxford, Oxford University Press.

Barr, J (1993b), Politics and the Bible, in B M Metzger and M D Coogan (eds), *The Oxford Companion to the Bible*, Oxford, Oxford University Press.

Barrett, C K (1955), *The Gospel according to St John*, London, SPCK.

Beckwith, R T (1993), Canon of the Hebrew Bible and the Old Testament, in B M Metzger and M D Coogan (eds), *The Oxford Companion to the Bible*, Oxford, Oxford University Press.

Bentley, J H (1993), Interpretation, history of: Christian interpretation from the Middle Ages to the Reformation, in B M Metzger and M D Coogan (eds), *The Oxford Companion to the Bible*, Oxford, Oxford University Press.

Best, E (1981), *Following Jesus: Discipleship in the Gospel of Mark*, Sheffield, JSOT Press.

Boerma, C (1979), *Rich Man, Poor Man and the Bible*, London, SCM.

Brown, R E (1971), *The Gospel According to John: translation and notes*, London, Geoffrey Chapman.

Brueggemann, W (1997), *Theology of the Old Testament: testimony, dispute, advocacy*, Minneapolis, Minnesota, Fortress Press.

Clines, D (1993), Possibilities and priorities of biblical interpretation in an international perspective, *Biblical Interpretation*, 1, 66–87.

Davies, P R (1995), *Whose Bible is it Anyway?* Sheffield, Sheffield Academic Press.

du Toit, A B (1993), Canon: New Testament, in B M Metzger and M D Coogan (eds), *The Oxford Companion to the Bible*, Oxford, Oxford University Press.

Fackenheim, E L (1990), *The Jewish Bible after the Holocaust: a Rereading*, Manchester, Manchester University Press.

Fawcett, R (1970), *The Symbolic Language of Religion: an introductory study*, London, SCM.

Fiorenza, E S (1993), *Revelation: vision of a just world*, Edinburgh, T and T Clark.

Froehlich, K (1993), Early Christian interpretation, in B M Metzger and M D Coogan (eds), *The Oxford Companion to the Bible*, Oxford, Oxford University Press.

Froehlich, K (1993), Interpretation, history of: Early Christian interpretation, in B M Metzger and M D Coogan (eds), *The Oxford Companion to the Bible*, Oxford, Oxford University Press.

Fuller, R H (1954), *The Mission and Achievement of Jesus*, London, SCM.

Hengel, M (1985), *Studies in the Gospel of Mark*, London, SCM.

Holbert, J C (1996), Deliverance belongs to Yahweh!: satire in the Book of Jonah, in P R Davies (ed.), *The Prophets: a Sheffield reader*, Sheffield, Sheffield Academic Press.

Hooker, M D (1983), *The Message of Mark*, London, Epworth Press.

Hooker, M D (1991), *A Commentary on the Gospel according to St Mark*, London, A and C Black.

Hooker, M D (1993), Mark, the Gospel according to, in B M Metzger and M D Coogan (eds), *The Oxford Companion to the Bible*, Oxford, Oxford University Press.

Isaacs, M E (1991), Exegesis and homiletics, *The Way: supplement on spirituality and scripture*, 72, 32–47.

Jeanrond, W G (1991), *Theological Hermeneutics: development and significance*, Basingstoke, Macmillan.

Lane, W (1974), *The Gospel according to Mark*, Grand Rapids, Michigan, Eerdmans.

Myers, C (1988), *Binding the Strong Man: a political reading of Mark's story of Jesus*, Maryknoll, New York, Orbis Books.

Myers, C, Dennis, M, Nangle, J, Moe-Lobeda, C and Taylor, S. (1996), *Say to this Mountain: Mark's story of discipleship*, Maryknoll, New York, Orbis Books.

Nineham, D E (1992), *The Gospel of St Mark*, Harmondsworth, Penguin.

Noll, M A (1991), *Between Faith and Criticism: evangelicals, scholarship and the Bible*, Leicester, Apollos.

Robinson, A T (1977), *Can We Trust the New Testament?* London, Mowbray.

Schweitzer, Albert (1998), *The Quest for the Historical Jesus*, Theissen and Merz.

Schweizer, E (1971), *The Good News according to Mark*, London, SPCK.

Stein, R H (1993), Parables, in B M Metzger and M D Coogan (eds) *The Oxford Companion to the Bible*, Oxford, Oxford University Press.

Streeter, B H (1924), *The Four Gospels: a study of origins*, London, MacMillan.

Theissen, G and Merz, A (1998), *The Historical Jesus: a comprehensive guide*, London, SCM.

Trible, P (1990), Feminist hermeneutics and biblical studies, in A Loades (ed.), *Feminist Theology: a reader*, London, SPCK.

Tuckett, C (1987), *Reading the New Testament: methods of interpretation*, London, SPCK.

Tyrell, G (1910), *Christianity at the Cross-roads*, London, Longmans.

Vidler, A R (1974), *The Church in an Age of Revolution: 1789 to the present day*, Harmondsworth, Penguin.

Watson, F (1994), *Text, Church and World: biblical interpretation in theological perspective*, Edinburgh, T and T Clark.

Ziesler, J A (1990), *Pauline Christianity* (revised edition), Oxford, Oxford University Press.

Applying for the Church Colleges' Certificate Programme

The certificate programme is available in Anglican Church Colleges of Higher Education throughout England and Wales. There are currently hundreds of students on this programme, many with no previous experience of study of this kind. There are no entry requirements. Some people choose to take Certificate courses for their own interest and personal growth, others take these courses as part of their training for ministry in the church. Some go on to complete the optional assignments and, after the successful completion of three courses, gain the Certificate. Courses available through the *Exploring Faith: theology for life* series are ideal for establishing ability and potential for studying theology and biblical studies at degree level, and they provide credit onto degree programmes.

For further details of the Church Colleges' Certificate programme, related to this series, please contact the person responsible for Adult Education in your local diocese or one of the colleges at the addresses provided:

The Administrator of Part-time Programmes, Department of Theology and Religious Studies, Chester College, Parkgate Road, CHESTER, CH1 4BJ ☎ 01244 375444

The Registry, Roehampton Institute, Froebel College, Roehampton Lane, LONDON, SW15 5PJ ☎ 0181 392 3087

The Registry, Canterbury Christ Church University College, North Holmes Road, CANTERBURY, CT1 1QU ☎ 01227 767700

The Registry, College of St Mark and St John, Derriford Road, PLYMOUTH, PL6 8BH ☎ 01752 636892

The Registry, Trinity College, CARMARTHEN, Carmarthenshire, SA31 3EP ☎ 01267 676804 (direct)

Church Colleges' Programme, The Registry, King Alfred's College, Sparkford Road, WINCHESTER, SO22 4NR ☎ 01962 841515

Part-time Programmes, The Registry, College of St Martin, Bowerham Road, LANCASTER, LA1 3JD ☎ 01524 384529